Advance Praise

"*Making the Low Notes* is a rollicking and heartfelt memoir about a lifelong love affair with music. Harrison writes about the highs and lows of a musician's life with wit, candor, and verve, capturing the pleasures of performing in the limelight as well as in its lambent periphery."

—**Meghan O'Gieblyn**, author of *Altered States* and *God, Human, Animal, Machine*

"Bill Harrison's memoir captures the wild life of a professional musician with great flair. I had a blast discovering the lessons Bill learned from Joe Daley, Warren Benfield, and other Chicago musical legends. Bill paints a vivid picture of the highs and lows of the circuitous path of the professional musician. Highly recommended!"

—**Jason Heath**, bassist, teacher, podcaster (*Contrabass Conversations*) and writer (*Double Bass Blog*)

"The artist's life is one of constant reinvention. In this vivid and candid tale, Bill Harrison's journey through that life visits the crazy, the difficult, and ultimately the rewarding places that are so common to this adventure. Readers in and out of the arts will recognize both the radical changes in the 'business' from the '60s to the nows, and the phases of life as one matures their way through it all. The tale of a true survivor, this deeply felt memoir transcends jazz bass, as does this next chapter of his own life."

—**Steve Rodby**, multi Grammy Award–winning bassist, producer, former member of the Pat Metheny Group

"I first met Bill Harrison nearly 50 years ago—when invited to hear the college quartet he writes about in the early chapters—and I got to see him play bass on stage often after that. But I never really *heard* him until reading this account of his honest, intimate, often witty and always insightful journey. Harrison takes us from his days as a lackadaisical student to sedulous accompanist to compassionate psychotherapist, aided first and foremost by taking stock of his own wrong turns. His lively writing contains a wealth of detail about the musicians' life, the gifted oddballs that line the path, and the pure joy of true collaboration. Title notwithstanding, Harrison hits plenty of high notes along the way."

—**Neil Tesser**, Grammy-winning author and broadcaster

"Harrison's memoir will tell you a lot about the bass and being a bassist, but his real themes include the development of a sensibility, the dignity of work, and how to do change. Although Harrison's knowledge of his instrument and the bassist's trade is bottomless (and delightful), he fetishizes neither. This is a profound book about life, love, and commitment."

—**David Van Biema**, former religion writer for *Time* magazine and coauthor of *The Prayer Wheel: A Daily Guide to Renewing Your Faith with a Rediscovered Spiritual Practice*

"Bill Harrison is an awesome, creative musician, a master of all styles of improvisation."

—**Hankus Netsky,** multi-instrumentalist, composer, faculty New England Conservatory

Making
the
Low
Notes

Making
THE
Low
Notes

a life in music

Bill Harrison

Open Books Press
Saint Louis, Missouri

Published by Open Books Press, USA

www.OpenBooksPress.com
info@OpenBooksPress.com

An imprint of Pen & Publish, LLC
www.PenandPublish.com
Saint Louis, Missouri
(314) 827-6567

Print ISBN: 978-1-956897-28-9
eBook ISBN: 978-1-956897-29-6

Library of Congress Control Number: 2022951054

Credit for epigraph on "Discord, Disunity, Gratitude, and Mercy":
Tony Hoagland, excerpt from "Special Problems in Vocabulary"
from *Application for Release from the Dream*. Copyright © 2015 by
Tony Hoagland. Reprinted with the permission of The Permissions
Company, LLC on behalf of Graywolf Press, Minneapolis, Minnesota,
graywolfpress.org.

Cover photos by Andrew McKone

for
Kelly Sill
(1952–2022)
bassist, raconteur, mentor

It is a joy to be hidden, but a disaster not to be found.

—D. W. Winnicott, *Playing and Reality*, 1971

Being born is the work of a lifetime.

—Allan Schnarr, MDiv, PhD, FeelingEverything.com

Contents

Part III

Part IV

A Note to the Reader

All the characters in this book are real flesh-and-blood humans. I use people's full names when I was certain no harm would come to them or when the person is deceased. Otherwise, I use first names only to protect people's privacy. I note in the text when I'm using a pseudonym.

Since this book is primarily about my life as a musician, I've chosen to exclude details of my family life, insofar as possible. I refer to relatives only when necessary for context and I've been deliberately circumspect regarding my children and other close family members.

Since trundling off to college in 1974, I've lugged around a ragged, musty cardboard box jammed with datebooks. I'm missing a year here and there but, for the most part, I have a written record of every gig, rehearsal, social occasion, lesson (taken and given), trip, visit from family, moving date, and most every other notable event that occurred between 1974 and 2010. I switched to using digital calendars in 2011, so I have access to the last decade's happenings as well, courtesy of Dr. Google.

I didn't hang on to this weighty pile of calendars for any conscious purpose. I wasn't keeping them because I'm nostalgic for "the good old days." Quite the contrary. I certainly never imagined I'd write a book.

Yet here we are.

Those planners came in mighty handy as I sought to verify dates and refresh my often-faulty memories of certain pivotal events. Among other surprises, I was startled to see names of people I hadn't thought about for decades—colleagues, students, bandleaders, mentors, friends, and too many people who are no longer with us.

You'll meet a few of these folks in the pages that follow.

Part I

Prelude

July 24, 1968

I'm rocking from foot to foot in the wings of my middle school auditorium's stage, clutching a double bass with both arms. Kids shuffle on and off stage, toting trumpets, trombones, clarinets, and flutes. So many flutes. When it's my turn, I death-grip the oversized fiddle and waddle into the spotlight.

My right hand is all slip and slide as I struggle to settle the bow on the string. I grab the neck of this beast with my left and plunge headlong into my rendition of "Yankee Doodle." It sounds like a nanny goat with an upset stomach. Then it's all over. Shocking applause erupts as I stumble offstage in a sweat-drenched daze.

I am never, ever doing this again.

And yet, as I retreat to the bosom of backstage, a wave of pleasure pulses through my body. Those moms and dads were applauding *for me*. Was that jolt of approval worth the jazzed-up breath, the jittery hands, the jumping-bean heart?

This is the intractable dilemma I would grapple with for the next four decades.

Billy's Choices

1967–1970

It was a glorious and formidable thing, a gleaming paisley of red, black, and white, with wide black leather straps that hugged my shoulders like a close friend. It had a 4-octave keyboard and 120 bass buttons. I'd been longing for an accordion ever since the afternoon in fourth grade when my fellow Cub Scout, Harris Ruderman, had carted his to a den meeting. All eyes were glued on him as he oom-pahed his way through a couple of lively tunes. I watched this weaselly stump of a kid magically transform into a celebrity, all because he could play an instrument.

I wanted to be cool like Ruderman so I began pestering my parents to buy me an accordion too. I imagined them *kvelling* as I squeezed out spirited versions of "Hava Nagila" at family gatherings. I dreamed that the girls at school (especially that cute redhead, Karen) would fall in love with me and that the boys would *plotz* with envy at my newfound musical superpowers.

At the time, my family—mother Barbara, father Bernie, sister Betty, and I—lived in Flushing, New York, perhaps the most appropriately named section of Queens. We'd be gone from there before my very own magnificent squeezebox would appear.

I was regularly shoved around the Andrew Jackson Elementary School (PS 24) schoolyard by some of the older kids. I was a year younger than most of my classmates, shy, asthmatic, and pudgy, attributes that didn't exactly work in my favor. They called me fatso, Jew boy, and faggot. Once a classmate stuck his face right up to mine, scrunched up the corners of his eyes, and hissed, "You're Chinese, aren't you?" I took refuge in Cub Scouts and in playing baseball with Jay, Arnie, Richie, and Andy at the scruffy park down the street.

Notwithstanding my playground woes, Mom always insisted I was an upbeat kid. I, however, remember wishing to be either invisible or Superman. Or both. In third grade, I would sometimes wear my Superman Halloween costume (including the red nylon cape) underneath my school clothes. I'd ask for a hall pass, then run to the boys' bathroom. Once there I'd pretend to shed my shirt and trousers before flying off to beat up some bad guys in Metropolis. Clark Kent's ability to hide his identity in plain sight was the emotional sweet spot I so desired.

At the age of eleven, I had chance to be a quasi-hero in real life. My family had moved from a medium-rise project to the top floor of a two-flat closer to PS 24. One night, Mom and Dad hired Joel, a teen from two doors down, to babysit Betty and me while they went to a party. I was drifting off to sleep when I became aware of waves of gray fluff hovering near the ceiling of my bedroom. My chest thwacked like a bass drum as I poked my head outside the doorway. Angry bursts of blackness billowed from behind the refrigerator. I tiptoed around the smoke and into the living room, where the babysitter was watching TV.

"Uh, Joel? Could you come in here?"

"Holy shit!" he shrieked as soon as he saw the surging soot. "Wake up your sister and let's get outta here."

A minute later the three of us were fumbling downstairs as the landlord came roaring out of the garage.

"The goddamn place is on fire!"

Betty and I spent the rest of the evening huddled on Joel's family's couch, trying to calm down as we waited for our parents to return. I couldn't bear to contemplate what might have happened had I not sensed the malevolent clouds in my bedroom.

Next morning, my family crept upstairs to inspect the remains of our possessions. Nearly everything was either burnt or waterlogged beyond salvaging. My eyes stung as we saw how the blaze had gutted our home. The charred rotten-egg stench of its aftermath is forever stored in my limbic system.

Within days, our family limped to a furnished apartment in a nearby high-rise so Betty and I could finish out the school year at PS 24. Barbara and Bernie were then faced with a decision they'd been putting off for some time: Should they rent another apartment in Flushing or make the leap to suburban homeownership?

For better or worse, they opted for the latter. They bought a house in Tenafly, New Jersey, a small upscale town across the Hudson from Manhattan. My stomach flopped at the thought of entering sixth grade in some strange school where I wouldn't know a soul.

It all happened in a whirlwind: the fire, the move to the shabby high-rise apartment, and now this—a three-story white frame house with hedges in the front yard, rosebushes in the back, and a garage. Our new home was disconcertingly opulent. If I'd had my druthers, we'd have remained in Queens, near my friends, as well as PS 24, the candy store on the corner, and the A&P on Kissena Blvd. It was far from paradise but at least I knew who I was in relation to those kids and places. Better to stay put than face the frightening unknowns of this disorienting place.

I understand now that children thrive with the familiar and resist change, even if the new is demonstrably better than the old. No one could have convinced me then that this move was an improvement.

The accordion showed up shortly after the move to Tenafly. I'd been badgering my folks about it for several years already, so why now? Perhaps the instrument was an appeasement for having to tolerate all the unwanted changes.

Mom signed me up for lessons with Marcello Roviaro, whose ever-present cardigans make me think of him as the Mr. Rogers of the accordion. With his thinning silver hair and wire-rimmed glasses, Mr. Roviaro looked ancient to me, though he couldn't have been much older than fifty at the time. He lived with his mother and brother. Mrs. Roviaro answered the phone with a heavy Italian accent whenever I called to cancel an upcoming lesson, usually feigning illness to cover for my wretched practice habits. I thought I was cleverly hiding my indolence, but of course, I was only fooling myself.

Mr. Roviaro was an even-tempered and patient fellow. The one time he became irritated was when he was offended by some chord changes in the Lennon/McCartney song "Day Tripper," which I'd brought in to learn.

"They have *no right* to do that," he sputtered through gritted teeth. To Mr. Roviaro, harmony had to obey certain rules. The Beatles apparently had subversive ideas about chords, which made me love them all the more.

I learned how to operate the piano-like keyboard with my right hand, the buttons with my left, and the bellows (the instrument's "lungs") with my left arm. Mr. Roviaro taught me the basics of reading music as well as the fingerings for all the major and minor scales. Playing accordion revealed my surprising natural ability to keep a steady tempo, a crucial skill for any musician. I'd come to appreciate this early training in later years. My family would *shep nachas*[1] when I'd play "Lady of Spain" or "The Beer Barrel Polka" for them.

Meanwhile, my days were taken up with finding my way in this strange new suburban world. On my first day at Tenafly Middle School, Mom drove me to a three-story red brick building fronted by technicolor trees and actual grass. Where was the cracked blacktop, the chain-link fence, the graffiti?

I bounced out of the car with a green canvas backpack hanging off one shoulder. I'd carefully packed it with sharpened No. 2 pencils, blue Bic pens, and a loose-leaf notebook filled with sweet-smelling lined paper. Not knowing any better, I wore my PS 24 uniform— black trousers with a short-sleeved white shirt and a striped clip-on tie. I strode toward the nearest entrance, a jaunty Poindexter, swinging my shiny Batman lunchbox.

"Go get 'em, tiger!" yelled a voice somewhere to my left. I turned and saw a group of older boys, laughing and thumbing in my direction. I pretended not to hear them and ran up the stairs in search of my homeroom.

All sixth graders had to take some kind of music class—band, orchestra, choir, or music appreciation. I'd been playing the accordion for a few months, but that wasn't going to help me at school. The thought of singing in a choir made me want to put a paper bag over my head. And I didn't need to be told that music appreciation (aka Mozart for Morons) was super dorky. The only viable alternative was to pick an instrument I could play in an ensemble, where I could tuck myself safely out of harm's way. And maybe find a new friend or two.

---

1   To derive pride and joy from another's accomplishments, often applied to one's children or grandchildren.

One morning that autumn, I ventured into the school's cavernous band room to meet with Mr. Wallin, Tenafly Middle School's music director.

"OK, Billy. What instrument would you like to try?"

"I wanna play the drums," I blurted, imagining myself as the next Ringo.

"Nah, sorry. We already have too many drummers."

I tried to hide my disappointment by staring at my Keds.

"Look, you can either play a brass instrument or one of those."

Mr. Wallin gestured toward three huge stringed things with giraffe necks lounging on a rack in a corner of the rehearsal room. Guitars for giants, maybe?

"Brass instrument?" I ventured.

"Yeah, like trumpet or trombone. Or maybe the sousaphone?"

I knew about the trumpet. My dad pulled his out of the hall closet once in a while and blatted a few notes. It made a farting sound. No, definitely not that. Trombone? Susie what? I shrugged.

"Uh, how about one of those?"

"Good choice."

"What are they?"

"They're double basses. Let's go pick one out for you."

My early weeks with the bass were a tough slog. The thing towered over me like Frankenstein's monster, its plywood body wide and unwieldy. The instrument seemed to get a kick out of messing with me. It kept keeling over when I tried to balance it between my left knee and my abdomen, as Mr. Wallin had instructed. He hovered nearby during lessons, a gymnastics spotter with Beethoven hair, ready to snag the bass whenever it got out of hand—or leg, as the case may be.

"Don't worry, Billy. You'll get the hang of it."

I wasn't so sure. Stretching the fingers of my left hand wide enough to play the notes more or less in tune was a torture worthy of Torquemada. Pushing the rope-like strings all the way down to the fingerboard required brawn I couldn't imagine having. My right thumb ached for weeks after Mr. Wallin showed me how to hold a bow. I learned the anatomy of my hands by way of pain during those first several months battling the bass. The persistent soreness made me want to throw in the towel, but I kept at it. No way was I going to give up and have to suffer the indignities of choir or music appreciation.

There was something besides avoiding those classes motivating me to endure the growth pangs of becoming a bass player: these lessons guaranteed me a spot in the school orchestra, which meant getting to hang out with girls. Naturally, there were girls in all my classes, but they were slightly less terrifying holding a violin or a flute, as long as the bass was firmly planted between them and me.

The afternoon I brought the school bass home for the first time, my mother and I shared a few befuddled minutes trying to decide how best to fit that enormous creature into her 1966 Ford Galaxie 500.

"Mr. Wallin said to swing it over the top of the passenger seat and rest the bottom part near the back window."

"Well, I don't see how that's possible," Mom said, pacing back and forth on the sidewalk, Marlboro in one hand, the other hand on her hip.

Our solution was to stow it in the back seat on its side with the neck protruding out the window. I later learned this is the most dangerous way to transport a bass.

When my dad saw the instrument in my room that evening, he dropped his voice à la Bela Lugosi and intoned, "I'm feelin' mighty low."

As middle school progressed, I realized there was nothing cool about the accordion or, for that matter, Harris Ruderman. The instrument's cachet had sunk like a waterlogged sousaphone with the ascension of rock'n'roll's iconic axe, the electric guitar. I'd already been keeping my accordion-playing proclivities confidential out of a reasonable fear that disclosure would destroy whatever social capital I'd managed to earn by then. Before the end of eighth grade I stopped visiting Mr. Roviaro's house and the squeezebox was relegated to its valise with the purple faux-velvet lining.

Choosing to play the bass in lieu of the accordion raised two generations of familial eyebrows.

"You gonna play 'Dayenu' on your bass fiddle at Passover?" Pop-Pop Moe asked. "Nobody will be able to sing along with that."

He had a point. The accordion puts its player front and center, with its ability to play melody, harmony, and rhythm simultaneously. Part of me ached for that attention; it's what lured me to the accordion in the first place. Another part of me sought the safety of the sidelines. The bass's primary role is to accompany other musicians rather than lead the way, which was a more inviting path for the budding introvert in me.

"It's hard to explain, Pop. I just feel more comfortable with the bass."

My parents questioned my choosing the bass over the accordion as well.

"We got you that beautiful instrument," my mother told me. "And Mr. Roviaro says you're doing real well with your lessons."

"I know, I know," I answered. "I'm sorry. I . . . I just don't like it anymore."

That wasn't entirely true but I couldn't articulate why I preferred to play a less visible, more supportive instrument. I intuited that my niche was in the shadows, where I could be a musical Clark Kent.

Six months into my tutelage with him, Mr. Wallin invited me to participate in that fateful recital in the summer of '68, where I performed solo in front of an audience for the first time. Throughout middle school, he took me as far along as a non-string player's teaching skills could go. If I was going to develop any further as a bassist—not a done deal by any stretch—I was going to have to find a real bass teacher.

The Tenafly Music Workshop
Summer School
Wednesday Evening, July 24, 1968

PART I - BEGINNERS

London Bridge
Jingle Bells
Twinkle, Twinkle Little Star
           Beginning Orchestra

Good-Nite Ladies	Gary Deeb, Trumpet
O, Come All Ye Faithful	Mark deSolminihac, Clarinet
Billy Boy	Neil Beshers, Trombone
Dick and Jane	Claire Rauscher, Sue Shaw
	Lissa Bloch, Debbie Kosman
Yankee Doodle	William Harrison, Bass Viol
Faith of our Fathers	Brian Green, Trumpet

Old MacDonald
Organ Reverie
Marines' Hymn
           Beginning Orchestra

To Have, to Hold, and to Hide

1969

To the best of my knowledge, an oboe is an oboe and a French horn is a French horn, but the granddaddy of the string family is known by over a dozen names: double bass, contrabass, bass fiddle, bull fiddle, bass violin, doghouse, big dog, bass viol, upright bass, acoustic bass, standup bass, slap bass, hoss bass, bunkhouse bass, and plain-old bass.

Whatever you call it, the bass is an imposing instrument. Even the smallest bass dwarfs its nearest relative, the cello. When you carry an upright bass, you know you're handling something substantial. They're not so much heavy as dense. Bulky. Awkward to maneuver. In playing position, whether the bassist stands or sits, the peg box and scroll hang in the air above the player's head.

My father thought the bass was shaped like a woman.

"I mean, look at it. The top part, what's that called?"

"The upper bout."

"Yeah, the upper bout looks like a buxom bosom. Check out that tiny waist around the bridge. And that bottom part—I bet it's called the lower bout—is shaped like nice meaty hips and a caboose."

Thank you, Dr. Freud. The bass might have a feminine shape, but the heft and sound suggest the masculine to me. I suppose it's possible the instrument's complex allusions to sexuality played a role in my choosing it over the brass instruments, but if so, that aspect was buried deep in my unconscious.

It's odd that there are so many monikers for an instrument that typically serves a secondary role to the flashier, single-named instruments like the violin, guitar, or saxophone. The bass is big for a reason: its range is lower than almost all other instruments and those low pitches require long, thick strings and a large enough chamber for them to resonate in. More often than not, the bass plays the lowest note in the band or orchestra, serving as a kind of sonic home base. The bass's low notes lie underneath it all, like the foundation of a building or the core of the Earth.

I recognized one particular benefit of the bass's size and shape right away: I could hide behind it. My face and hands were visible, of course, but if I held the bass just so, I could use it to shield my body from view. Again, I don't imagine I grokked this when I told Mr. Wallin I'd like to try playing this instrument. But hiding behind the bass suited my middle school personality to a T.

Sex, Drugs, Blisters, and Beethoven

1970–1974

Music wasn't a priority in the Harrison household. My father Bernie had messed around with the aforementioned fart producer as a teenager, including a summer spent entertaining the *zaydes* and *bubbes* at a resort in the Catskills. My mother Barbara had briefly sawed on the viola in junior high. By the time I came along in 1956, my parents' interest in playing music had been supplanted by the practical concerns of making a living and raising my sister and me. When Betty and I were in single digits, our family didn't attend concerts or gather 'round the old hi-fi to listen to records or the radio. Unlike many of my future colleagues, I wasn't immersed in music from early on.

We did, however, see musicals, live and on film, throughout my childhood. I'd sing along with recordings of *Fiddler on the Roof*, *Mary Poppins*, *The Sound of Music*, *The Jungle Book*, and *Dumbo* when I was alone. Someone gave me a picture book with a set of 45s from the pachyderm movie, which I wore out on my portable record player with the yellow plastic tonearm. (I didn't get how racist that movie was until much later in life.)

One afternoon when I was around twelve, I was rummaging around the basement for something when I was astonished to discover my father's stash of dusty LPs. Among other things, Dad owned a set of the legendary Toscanini/NBC Symphony recordings of all nine Beethoven symphonies, with their forest-green sleeves and raised gold lettering. When had any of these discs last been played? My curiosity piqued, I listened to them repeatedly over the next several weeks. Beethoven opened my ears to the power of harmony and orchestration in ways musicals never could have.

Similar serendipitous forces must have drawn me toward the double bass LPs at Sam Goody's one day in ninth grade. I normally haunted the rock racks, looking for albums by my favorite groups: Creedence Clearwater Revival, Santana, Led Zeppelin, Traffic, Jethro Tull, and of course, the Beatles. There was nothing new in that department, so I wandered over to uncharted territory—the classical bins. I left the store with a life-altering gem.

As soon as I got the record unwrapped at home I dropped the needle on the first track of *Gary Karr Plays Double Bass*. From the first notes of Henry Eccles's "Sonata in G Minor," Karr's playing was a revelation. This is how a bass can sound, focused and bright, not gruff and muddy? How does he play so fast? And so amazingly in tune?

Karr was a *wunderkind* who made his debut in 1962 at the age of twenty-one with Leonard Bernstein and the New York Philharmonic, performing Saint-Saëns's "The Swan" on television. He was descended from seven generations of bassists, a familial oddity that ought to be in the *Guinness Book of World Records*. Almost overnight, Karr became a sensation in the classical music world, especially (and unsurprisingly) among bass players. His razor-sharp tone, dramatic vibrato, and uncommonly wide range of dynamics distinguished him from previous bass virtuosi—a rare breed of bird to begin with. By the time Side One ended I'd found my double bass lodestar.

I was certainly no *wunderkind*. Gary Karr's virtuosity induced me to practice, albeit spottily, and inspired me to seek a bona fide bass instructor. I was talking with a friend about this quest in a hallway at school one day when a passerby overheard our conversation.

"Hey, Harrison, my father's a bass player," a voice behind me said. I wheeled around and encountered Sam Bruno, a kid I only knew as a tough guy who played football. He'd never spoken directly to me before.

"Oh, yeah?" I responded wittily. "Does he give lessons?"

"I dunno, but I could ask him."

"Man, that'd be great."

Sam nodded and took off without another word. I guess it wouldn't have been good for his reputation to be seen chatting with the nerdy likes of me. A few days later, Sam slipped me a scrap of paper on which he'd scrawled his phone number.

"My dad says you can call him if you like."

"OK, Sam. Thanks a lot."

He gave me a quick two-finger salute and disappeared.

Sam Bruno Sr. was kind of a tough guy too. With his slicked-back hair, furry oil-black eyebrows, and thick-framed glasses, he could have passed for Martin Scorsese's dangerous older brother. The index finger on Mr. Bruno's right hand stuck out stiffly, bent backwards at an impossible angle at the middle knuckle. This deformity must have been a huge obstacle to his playing career but he didn't talk about it. I don't know if it was a congenital condition or the result of some horrific accident. I was too intimidated to ask.

Mr. Bruno was a freelance bassist, who, like Gary Karr, hailed from a family of bass players. He had a sense of humor, but was no-nonsense when it came to musicianship and proper technique. I knew he meant business both by his demeanor and by the car he drove. Mr. B. got around in a Volkswagen Beetle from which he'd removed the passenger-side seat. His bass nestled in the empty cavity as if it had been custom-made.

Early in my studies with him, Mr. Bruno helped me find my first double bass, which my parents generously purchased. It was manufactured by Kay, the company that built some of the best plywood basses from the late 1930s until 1968, the year the business folded. I named my new bass Igor, because of the way it loomed in the corner of my bedroom like a monster. Igor wasn't a great instrument, except by comparison to the clunker I'd been wrestling with at school. That Kay was my intimate adversary for all the formative musical events of my youth. Wherever Igor is now, it bears the imprint of my adolescent sweat and blood. That's neither metaphor nor hyperbole.

Mr. Bruno taught me using the most common method book of that era, written by an evil bastard named Franz Simandl (1840–1912). Most bassists of a certain age have a love/hate relationship with his *New Method for the Double Bass*, but my feelings about it were straightforward: I loathed it. The etudes in the book were maddening, especially for a beginner. They didn't sound good, even when played well, although that's a summit I never attained.

Despite being a jazz and commercial bassist who made his living playing *pizzicato* ("with the fingers"), Mr. Bruno insisted I continue learning to play *arco* ("with the bow"). I was initially resistant to this idea because the bowed sound I produced resembled the croaking of distressed bullfrogs. For some reason, I could get a pretty robust sound playing *pizzicato*. That is, until the blisters erupted.

Blisters were the bane of my early bass-playing life, because plucking the strings causes friction normal fingertips aren't designed to endure. Those painful pockets of pus bloomed on the first two fingers of my right hand as the result of inconsistent practicing. The less I played regularly, the slower my fingers developed callouses, the only preventive for blisters.

My ardor for playing the bass wavered unpredictably; some days I was really into it, other times practicing was too steep a mountain to climb. I was also easily distracted, both by the usual pubescent preoccupations—girls, schoolwork, hanging around aimlessly with friends, and have I mentioned girls?—and by my two other adolescent passions, filmmaking and radio.

In eighth grade, my father gave me a Bolex Super 8 mm movie camera. I shot home movies with it, including several birthday parties and a "documentary" of a family trip to Yellowstone Park in 1973. I brought the camera with me to Beginners' Showcase, a summer drama camp in New Hampshire, where I created a disjointed, pretentious documentary set to Blind Faith's classic song "Do What You Like." The Bolex later got me into hot water during a high school band trip to Washington, DC.

Everything about filmmaking fascinated me: the scripts, the sets, the cameras, the lighting and audio gear, acting, editing, and directing.

Which is why my audio maven friend Phil and I produced what may have been the first ever *Star Trek* fan film. We adapted an episode from the original TV series and shot most of it in the Harrison family's basement, using the Bolex, a reel-to-reel tape deck, and a funky microphone duct-taped to a broomstick. The production was an all-consuming project for several months, the evidence of which is sadly no longer extant. Igor gathered dust in the corner of my bedroom for most of this period.

Radio broadcasting was the other magnetic distraction from practicing bass. In the '50s, '60s, and '70s—the Dark Ages before online streaming services—all popular music was disseminated via broadcast radio. Even the most successful groups like the Beatles and the Rolling Stones needed disc jockeys to help sell their records. When I was in elementary and middle school, most kids I knew listened to WABC-AM, New York's Top 40 rock'n'roll powerhouse. By high school, my peers and I had migrated to the FM dial. For music, WNEW-FM was the place to hear gravel-voiced Scott Muni spin records by Jefferson Airplane, Led Zeppelin, Mountain, Emerson, Lake and Palmer, Black Sabbath, and the other heavy groups of that era.

With the help of that same pal, Phil, I pieced together a makeshift radio studio in my family's basement/film studio, using a couple of salvaged turntables, a Radio Shack microphone, and a six-channel Shure mixer (another great gift from my father). I spent many late afternoons pretending to broadcast a show, spinning records and practicing my patter in between songs.

Though my parents disapproved, nearly every night between the ages of about twelve and sixteen, I stayed up past my bedtime listening to Jean Shepherd on WOR-AM. Shepherd was a humorist and raconteur who held forth on the radio and in books and magazine articles. His sardonic tone was a powerful influence on my teenaged world view. Shepherd's semi-autobiographical stories are set in the fictional town of Hohman, Indiana, a none-too-subtle analogue for Hammond, not far from Chicago, a city that would figure prominently in my life before long. My early attempts at creative writing owe more than a little to Shepherd's blend of humor and pathos. Now Shepherd is best known for writing the iconic holiday film *A Christmas Story*—the one with the "you'll shoot your eye out, kid" Red Ryder BB gun.

I couldn't decide if I wanted to play rock records like Scott Muni or tell stories like Jean Shepherd, but the radio bug bit me hard in adolescence. At fifteen, I studied for and earned my third-class FCC license (known as a "third phone"), which was required if you wanted to be on the air.

In retrospect, I can see how radio and filmmaking appealed to the same aspects of my personality that preferred the bass over the accordion. Nobody sees the person behind the microphone or the camera. I could do my thing but remain safely out of sight.

Of course, when I was making films or pretending to be a radio DJ, I wasn't practicing for my bass lessons with Mr. Bruno. He had to put up with a lot of indolence for his lousy $10 a lesson. Sorry, Mr. B., wherever you are.

Though it was an arduous undertaking, the upside of improving my *arco* technique was that it gave me the chance to play with a real orchestra. Early in the summer of 1970, my mother heard through the suburban moms' grapevine that a nearby youth orchestra needed some warm bodies to fill out their string section. She suggested I give it a go. I figured what the hell, why not?

I was unprepared for the polychromatic explosion of sound that enveloped me at the first rehearsal I attended with the Bergen Youth Orchestra.

Eugene Minor, BYO's aptly named music director, started us off with the opening movement of Beethoven's Symphony no. 3 (The "Heroic"). The piece begins with two massive Eb major chords, played by the entire orchestra. The oomph of those chords nearly made me jump out of my skin. Then, without further introduction, the cellos, who were sitting right in front of me, played the opening theme. I'd heard this piece before, but only on my Dad's crackly LP played through flimsy speakers. This was the real sonic deal—and I was right in the middle of it.

The Bergen Youth Orchestra was a full-sized symphony, unlike the puny ensembles in the Tenafly school system. These kids played in tune and with rhythmic vitality. Many of these students, with a few notable exceptions (ahem), were well on their way to professional-level competency. They had the chops to sound convincing performing some of the masterpieces in the standard orchestral literature by Beethoven, Dvorak, Tchaikovsky, and Mozart. Playing those glorious orchestrations sent shivers of electric energy through my nervous system.

After one rehearsal in late August, Maestro Minor took me aside.

"So, do you want to play with the orchestra during the school year?"

"Sure. Wait, do I have to audition?"

"No. I've heard you play, and I've talked it over with John. You're in if you want to be."

"Wow. Great. Thanks."

John was John Feeney, the exceptionally talented principal (leader) of BYO's bass section. John played the shit out of the same Eccles sonata that had so impressed me on that Gary Karr LP. The other guys (no girls, sigh) were solid bassists too. I gladly accepted my place at the rear of the bass section, where I could lurk and learn.

Mom drove me to and from BYO rehearsals, and both my parents attended every concert over the next four years. They weren't bass converts yet, but they could see I was semi-serious about music.

After one concert my father gave me his take on what he'd just heard.

"Y'know," he said. "I can't really hear the basses, but I can tell when you all *aren't* playing."

I'm still mulling that one over.

My membership in the BYO led to an invitation from Gene Minor to spend parts of two consecutive summers ('73 and '74) at Lighthouse Music and Art Camp. Situated in the Poconos near the town of Pine Grove, Pennsylvania, the place was teeming with overachieving students in, well, music and arts. I played in the camp orchestra, where I consistently lagged a few paces behind my peers. I was much more relaxed in the jazz band, where some mysterious instincts for that music kicked in.

But the most noteworthy lessons from those two summers were non-musical in nature.

Somebody blended a batch of Brandy Alexanders at a party I found myself at early the first summer. I drank one, mistaking it for an ice cream soda. I had no idea this concoction contained alcohol until I tried to stand up. The room lurched sideways as I clutched the nearest piece of furniture to prevent an undignified spill. First time drunk. Check.

I was riding in the back seat of an allegedly responsible adult's car one day when said adult broke out a small squeeze bottle of something he called poppers. The driver and the other two teen campers squeezed the bottle and inhaled, then passed the stuff to me.

"Do you have any heart problems?" asked the responsible adult.

"No, not that I know of," I said.

"OK. Well, give the bottle a little squirt as you inhale and you'll get off."

"Uh . . ."

"Well, you don't have to. More for us."

Everyone laughed. I was under the gun. I could sniff the poppers and be cool or I could cement my reputation as a square dork by refraining.

"No, I'm gonna try it," I said as gamely as I could manage.

I tipped my head back as I'd seen each of the others do and pulled the trigger.

"Nothing's happening," I said.

"Give it a second, will ya?" said the R.A.

Whoo! A jolt of something snapped through my head and chest. I can't say it was pleasant.

"There you go!" exclaimed one of the other passengers.

First time using a dangerous substance to get high. Check. I later learned that what we were huffing was amyl nitrate, an inhalant used by doctors to treat angina and by drug enthusiasts for a quick high and to enhance sexual pleasure. We were screwing around with stuff that shouldn't have been proffered to a fifteen-year-old. But this was the 1970s; what happened at music and art camp stayed at music and art camp.

During my second summer in Pine Grove, I saw a naked woman in the flesh for the first time. Check. She and a male camper were standing in the buff near the window of one of the cabins in the middle of a steamy afternoon. I was meandering by with a violinist friend, who was the first of us to catch a glimpse of the exposed skin a stone's throw to our left. We maturely dove behind some nearby bushes and gawked until the couple disappeared from view.

Two thoughts barreled through my brain simultaneously: *Oh my God, how fantastic is this* and *You should be ashamed of yourself for staring at that girl.* The fiddle player and I swore one another to secrecy, an oath I've not betrayed—until now.

Another time, I walked in on Andy, my trumpet-playing roommate, who was (I later figured out) playing strip poker with an attractive female camper. She was fully dressed; he was wearing nothing but a Yankees cap, socks, and sneakers. I guess that meant he was losing the game, but he was apparently winning in some other way, if his gigantic erection was any indication. Rather than scooting right back out the door, I plopped down on my cot for an excruciating moment before realizing I'd better skedaddle. I mumbled "Uh, sorry man," and beat it out of there. First (and last) time in the presence of another man's erect penis. Check.

I blame all of this delinquency on the bass.

Digging Sides with Korky

1970–1974

At first, playing with the Bergen Youth Orchestra filled my ears and brain with a kaleidoscope of fresh sensations. I anticipated concerts with excitement and trepidation in equal measure. Rehearsing and performing with the orchestra taught me how to listen to the ensemble as a whole and how to follow a conductor while reading a bass part, skills I'd come to value in later years. As my father had pointed out in his inimitable way, our bass section wielded unmistakable power. When we dug into a *fortissimo* passage, the resulting vibrations were seismic.

Over time, though, the downsides of orchestral playing began to gnaw at me.

During one Saturday afternoon rehearsal, Gene Minor was putting the orchestra's string section through its paces. We were trying to clean up the trio section from the third movement of Beethoven's Fifth Symphony, a notorious passage Ludwig apparently composed to expose the flaws of the cellos and basses. It was sounding like a bucket of mud.

"I appreciate the volume," our conductor said. "You know how much I love seeing clouds of rosin flying off your strings. But you're stomping on the articulation and intonation like a herd of elephants. Let's try it again with a bit more accuracy, *s'il vous plaît*."

I couldn't tell if I was in tune or not. Every note I played got sucked into the sonic vortex of the bass section. It was already a challenge blending with my compadres, but navigating the fingerboard using the Braille method frustrated me. We never got that Beethoven passage up to speed.

Another drawback was the rigid top-down hierarchy of the orchestra, which left little room for personal expression. Symphony orchestras are organized like corporations, with the conductor (Maestro Minor in our case) as CEO. Craig, our concertmaster, was COO; his job was to ensure that all the strings (violins, violas, cellos, and basses) toed the company line. Finally, each instrument's section has a straw boss, called the principal, who's charged with managing the individual players. John was cool but I still chafed at these layers of authority which made my musical input feel negligible.

On the one hand, I was safely cocooned in the back of the section. There were plenty of licks in those orchestral pieces I couldn't hack, and my position made it unlikely I'd ever be called out individually. On the other hand, I yearned for something more, something that felt more like *me*. This desire had echoes of the longing for attention that had drawn me to the accordion a few years earlier. Feeling safe and secure all the time wasn't enough anymore.

Jamming with my friends, Korky the pianist and Ted the saxophonist, was an antidote for this malaise. We'd gather in the high school's band room and let 'er rip, playing as long, loud, and crazy as we wanted. I'd work up a lather in no time, blood blisters be damned. None of us knew what the hell we were doing, flailing away on a single chord or copping a groove from a pop song like Traffic's "Feelin' Alright" and running it into the ground.

Like a young Isaac Newton getting bopped on the head with an apple, I experienced a revelation during our naïve musical meanderings: *There's only one bass player in a jazz group.* There's no competing to be heard over a batch of other bassists. Even our primitive improvising gave me the freedom to imbue the music with my personality.

The clouds parted and the angels sang: *This is what you've been looking for!* The fallen angels countered with: *What makes you think you have any business playing this music?*

One afternoon, Korky invited me over to his house to, as he put it, "check out some real jazz." Korky was a remarkable young man. He attracted a wide circle of friends with his unaffected charm and Mojave-dry sense of humor. His intellect far exceeded that of anyone else in my orbit—and I had some sharp friends. No one was surprised when he scored a perfect 1600 on the SAT. There was also something bittersweet in his disposition, as if he had already lived a long, sorrowful life. He certainly knew a helluva lot about jazz.

That afternoon, Korky gently placed a copy of Miles Davis's *Kind of Blue* on the turntable. The record opens with ethereal chords played by pianist Bill Evans. After a few seconds, bassist Paul Chambers states the melody of this composition, called "So What." I'll tell you what—*holy shit!* When the full band hit for the trumpet solo, I couldn't stop my head from bobbing to the infectious groove. Korky glanced at me with an impish smile. This Chambers guy swung like crazy. Miles played with sublime lyricism, alto saxophonist "Cannonball" Adderley's solo was steeped in the bebop tradition, and tenor player John Coltrane blew like a man on a mission to say it all right here and now. These men sounded like they were from different planets in the same solar system. I hadn't heard anything remotely like this before.

As I grew to know their music more intimately, Evans, Davis, and Coltrane became three of my jazz heroes. For the time being, though, I only had ears for Paul Chambers. His buoyant sound burrowed deep into my guts. His phenomenal solos, both *pizzicato* and *arco*, knocked me out. He was as impressive to me then as Gary Karr had been a couple of years earlier. This time, though, I could relate to the music on a more visceral level.

Korky was a devotee of so-called "free jazz" musicians like Albert Ayler, Art Ensemble of Chicago, Cecil Taylor, and Ornette Coleman. During one of our sessions digging sides (hipster parlance for listening to records), he nonchalantly picked up a shiny yellow two-LP set and said,

"You might like this bass player."

The album was *Paris Concert*, a live recording by a quartet called Circle, featuring saxophonist Anthony Braxton and a young pianist named Chick Corea. After the first track, a wild and wacky romp through the standard "There Is No Greater Love," the bassist played a seven-minute improvised solo piece called "Song for the Newborn." It was a *tour de force*.

"Who is this guy?"

"Dave Holland," Korky answered. "He's British. Miles heard him at Ronnie Scott's, a London jazz club, and asked him to join his band around 1968."

Holland's chops, his sound, his ability to create this stunning piece out of thin air, impressed me to no end. Dave's playing became my Kilimanjaro right then and there. And Korky, that sly trickster, knew that Circle's music would blow my mind.

When my friend mentioned that Dave Holland would be participating in a week-long series of lectures, demonstrations, and concerts in the spring of 1974, I heard the clarion call of opportunity. The Creative Music Studio would take place in New York City near the end of senior year, a time I expected would be a yawner. I petitioned my parents and the high school administrators for permission to sign up for the event and, after a bit of campaigning, the adults agreed to allow me to hang out at Artists' House (Ornette Coleman's performance space) in Greenwich Village.

Early afternoon each day, students would meander into 131 Prince Street, primed for whatever that day's session would bring. Percussionist Milford Graves led a class in collective improvisation; drummer Jack DeJohnette tried to teach us how to play in 7/4 time; composer Richard Teitelbaum immersed us in loud white noise for thirty minutes so we could observe how our minds would invent little melodies in the midst of that aural chaos. Composer George Russell presented a traditional lecture on his "Lydian Chromatic Concept of Tonal Organization." At the other end of the spectrum, saxophonist Sam Rivers let his horn do the talking.

Every day was jaw-dropping; I had no point of reference for any of this music or these people. It was heady stuff for a seventeen-year-old kid.

Much like my weeks at Lighthouse, my learning experiences at CMS went beyond the musical. One day, for instance, I nearly got punched out by bassist Sirone (aka Norris Jones) after a rehearsal he'd just played with the Revolutionary Ensemble. I'd stepped up to the table at the front of the room to buy one of the band's LPs when Sirone came at me. His face was contorted in a menacing grimace; his arms shook with fury.

"YOU! Hand over that tape recorder right now."

"I don't have a tape recorder," I replied, taking a step back.

"Man, I saw you holdin' a microphone and cuttin' down the volume on your recorder—five minutes ago!"

"Sir, you have the wrong guy. I don't even own a portable recorder."

Right then, Leroy Jenkins, the violinist and leader of the trio, stepped between us.

"Sirone. Man. Calm down. This young man is buying one of our records. He didn't do anything."

Saved by the fiddle player. Sirone would've flattened me easily. Now I conjecture that he may have been suffering from some mental health issues. In the moment, however, it was pure terror.

Dave Holland played three concerts during the workshop. I kicked myself for having to miss the first one, when Dave performed with Jack DeJohnette and guitarist John Abercrombie. He played the second night with vibist Karl Berger, the workshop's organizer, vocalist Ing Rid, and drummer Phil Wilson. I mustered the gumption to introduce myself to Dave during a break in their afternoon rehearsal.

"Your playing knocks me out," was all my nervous brain could come up with to blurt. "How do you do it?"

"Well," Dave said. "I work very hard."

"I thought maybe you'd discovered some magical secret to unlocking all the mysteries of the bass."

"No magic," he said with a laugh. "It takes a lot of time and concentrated effort. You've got to develop a sympathy for what's happening between your body and the bass—so you can relax and let the music flow."

For a second, I allowed myself to imagine what it might be like to achieve the kind of musical mastery I observed in Dave.

"Would you like to try out my bass?" Dave asked.

Hell yeah I would. Dave picked up his instrument and guided it carefully into my waiting arms. Great Caesar's ghost! This bass practically played itself. I'd have messed with it all day if he'd have let me.

"Woah, that's amazing."

"Yeah, she's a dandy, right?" Dave said, as he reached for the neck and took the bass out of my hands. That was a minute I'd never forget.

The closing night's concert was the one I'd been most eagerly anticipating. It featured Holland with Sam Rivers and Barry Altschul. Rivers, one of the most accomplished musicians of his era, played tenor sax, soprano sax, and flute. Altschul used an array of drums, cymbals, bells, and percussive toys. The trio played two long sets, each one a single free-flowing improvisation that moved in and out of various textures, tempos, and styles. It was as if these three musicians melded into one being. The connection between them was palpable, even to a neophyte like me.

"Words cannot express" was the only comment I made about this night in my notes. I didn't yet know what sex was like, but I couldn't imagine feeling any more elated than when I stumbled toward the subway after that gig.

Wrestling

1969–1974

During senior year of high school, Korky and I hung out some afternoons digging sides and playing piano/bass duets in his family's living room. Occasionally we took a stab at one of the tunes from *Kind of Blue* or a jazz standard, but mostly we improvised without referencing a song or any other predetermined material—our humble attempts at "free jazz."

We could play anything that popped into our minds at any moment. There were times when Korky and I seemed to be tuned into the same wavelength. We came up with some crazy-ass shit, and every once in a while, we inexplicably "found" the same notes or rhythms simultaneously. This was spooky and thrilling and deeply satisfying.

"What about Benny Goodman? Is that real jazz?" I asked Korky one day while we were taking a breather. "My father says Goodman had the best band."

"The best white band maybe," my friend answered. "I guess it was cool that he hired Lionel Hampton to integrate his quartet, but the music? I don't know. The Black big bands were the swingin'-est."

Wait, I thought. *There are Black bands and white bands?*

"What bands are you talking about?"

"Oh, Fletcher Henderson, Jimmy Lunceford, Earl Hines, Cab Calloway, Chick Webb, Count Basie, Duke Ellington."

"I've heard of Duke Ellington but I don't know those other names."

"That's the problem right there. Those musicians created the music that guys like Artie Shaw, Tommy Dorsey, Glenn Miller, and, yeah, Benny Goodman, copied and brought to white audiences."

I sat there, mute. I knew my parents had danced to Miller's and Dorsey's bands when they were courting in the 1950s. I knew my father liked Miles Davis and Al Hirt, but neither he nor Mom ever mentioned any of the bands Korky had named.

I realized in that moment that, with the exception of pianist Bill Evans, Miles's *Kind of Blue* band was all Black. The subsequent group the trumpeter put together in the '60s—Wayne Shorter (sax), Herbie Hancock (piano), Ron Carter (bass), and Tony Williams (drums)—was entirely African American. With the exception of Dave Holland, all the bass players I most admired, including Paul Chambers, Charles Mingus, and Ray Brown, were Black. Most of the contemporary jazz musicians who interested me were also African American: Ornette Coleman, Eric Dolphy, Freddie Hubbard, Bobby Hutcherson, McCoy Tyner, Joe Henderson, and Ed Blackwell. How could I have been so blind to this obvious racial dimension?

My friend loaned me a couple of Leroi Jones's books, *Blues People* and *Black Music*, which trace the history of the music from an Afrocentric perspective. I discovered that every style of jazz had originated with Black musicians. Louis Armstrong, Duke Ellington, Coleman Hawkins, Lester Young, Thelonious Monk, Charlie Parker, Dizzy Gillespie, among many others, were the innovators who propelled the music into new territory.

On Korky's recommendation, I also read A. B. Spellman's *Four Lives in the Bebop Business*, a volume that explores the hardships endured by some of the seminal Black jazz musicians of the time: saxophonists Jackie McLean and Ornette Coleman, and pianists Herbie Nichols and Cecil Taylor.

These bits of knowledge made me hungry for more. I devoured Richard Wright's *Black Boy*, Ralph Ellison's *Invisible Man*, *The Autobiography of Malcolm X*, Lorraine Hansberry's *A Raisin in the Sun*, Eldridge Cleaver's *Soul on Ice*, and the poetry of Amiri Baraka.

Before Korky opened my eyes and ears, I knew nothing about African American music and history. I loved the Beatles, the Rolling Stones, and Led Zeppelin without ever realizing that their music derived directly from the blues and other Black music.

My mother noticed my choice of listening and reading material.

"It looks like you're going through a Black phase," she said.

It's not a phase, I wanted to retort. *I'm learning about reality, stuff you and Dad never exposed me to. This ain't some* Oklahoma! *bullshit.*

The more I learned about African American culture, the worse I felt about being white and Jewish. I dug playing jazz, but as I educated myself about the music's history, I became convinced that only Black people could be real jazz musicians. I was *certain*, at the age of sixteen, that the best I could hope for would be to become skilled enough to hang out with the authentic cats. Not only would I never be anything but a dilettante, I thought, but my skin color and ethnic heritage also made me an unwitting accomplice to the oppressive majority.

I read about African American history and listened to Black music, but what did I know about non-white people in real life? Zilch, with the exception of one brief incident in middle school:

Coach Boaz "Buzz" Firkser grabs me by the front of my gym shirt and shoves me onto the wrestling mat. It looks like the jig is up. I've been hiding in the weeds for weeks, hoping to avoid this exact situation.

"Frank, get over here," he bellows.

You have got to be fucking kidding me.

Frank is the only Black kid in eighth grade—the only Black kid in our school, come to think of it. He's built like a Patton tank; I'm a flabby *nebbish*. Some of the other boys call him "Chip," a nickname I don't understand. And the coaches ride his ass more than they do the rest of us. That's all I know about Frank, except that I'm sure he's going to pummel the shit out of me. He and I have never exchanged a single word.

As I stumble onto the mat, I become aware that there's more at stake than mere humiliation. I'm a white Jewish kid facing a Black kid for a sanctioned brawl in a school gymnasium. I know it's not gonna happen, but how would it feel if I beat this kid, who's had a pretty tough go in our very white school? I'm sure of one thing: I want no part of this wrestling match.

"Billy, you're on top. Get down, Frank."

Frank crouches on all fours. I kneel next to him, place my left hand on his left elbow, and wrap my right arm around his back. I rest my hand oh-so-gently on his abdomen. My gut clenches; my heart slams.

"Ready . . . wrestle."

It all goes haywire in a heartbeat. Frank flips me like a flapjack and jams my shoulders into the mat. I'm flat on my back, wheezing. My arm feels like it's been wrenched from its socket. My mouth fills with the gray taste of shame.

Guess I didn't need to worry about winning.

Frank and I never discussed what happened that day. We were thirteen-year-old boys. We could fight but we couldn't talk.

Most of the other children in the New York City public schools I'd attended in the '60s were, to the best of my recollection, some variety of white. All my teachers were white women. So the idea that white is "normal" was the only reality I'd ever known. It's possible that there were more Black and Latino kids than I remember and that they were invisible from inside my cozy white bubble.

There was a handful of non-white kids at my suburban middle school. I know now that they were mostly East Asian and Latino, but their names just sounded weird to me at the time. They kept to themselves, and were largely ignored by my white classmates. I don't recall if I actively contributed to the social isolation we imposed on those kids, but I certainly didn't reach out to befriend any of them.

So when Korky was schooling me on the Black musicians who were masters of the music I wanted to play, I asked him, "What does this all mean for white jazz players?"

"Well, there are plenty of excellent musicians of the Caucasian persuasion," my friend said. "Stan Getz, Chet Baker, Buddy Rich, Charlie Haden—a great bass player, by the way—Paul Bley, Jim Hall..."

"So it's OK for us to play jazz then?"

I knew it was a stupid question as soon as the words tumbled out of my mouth. Korky gave me one of his "do you realize how naïve you're being right now" looks. Though I couldn't yet know how I'd feel or behave when wrestling with racism in the future, I promised myself I'd continue listening, learning, and checking myself so I wouldn't always be so damn clueless.

A Wedding

1970

There's an old joke about a young bass player whose father sends him for his first lesson with the local bass teacher.

"How'd it go?" the father asks.

"Great!" the son says. "I learned how to play C and G."

A week later the father gets a call from the teacher saying his kid didn't show up for his second lesson. When the boy gets home, his dad asks him why he didn't go to his lesson.

"Because I got a gig."

In case you don't get it, the joke is that the bass is allegedly so easy to play that anyone can score a gig after learning how to play only two notes.

My tenor saxophone–playing friend Ted hired me for my first-ever paying gig during freshman year of high school. Or it might have been Korky who did the hiring. Either way, the three of us, plus a drummer whose name and face I've forgotten, were contracted to play a wedding reception. In a *bowling alley*.

Our quartet rehearsed diligently before the job. The set list included "The Girl from Ipanema," "Satin Doll," "Misty," and two contemporary numbers, "Bad, Bad Leroy Brown" and "Joy to the World" (Three Dog Night, not G. F. Handel). We probably knew how to play a twelve-bar blues by then, but I can't imagine we knew any other actual songs, so we must have milked those five tunes dry to get through the gig. My immature bass chops were no match for the clattering of bowling pins combined with the racket my bandmates produced. I survived the gig, with the inevitable blood blisters on the fingertips of my right hand. I think we each took home $15, which means whoever hired a bunch of high school kids for the biggest day of their life got exactly what they paid for.

As odd as the venue was, perhaps a bowling alley was an appropriate place for my maiden voyage as a professional musician. I didn't know it yet, but my ever-simmering internal conflict between competing desires—to be seen and heard versus hidden and ashamed—would sometimes manifest as grandiosity. The absence of appropriate humility would get in the way of my growth as a musician and as a human.

I'm hard pressed to imagine a humbler venue for a first gig than among the lanes and pins. I wish I'd used it as a reminder to keep my defensive arrogance in check.

A Musical and a Parade

1970–1974

Throughout most of middle and high school I had a dreadful crush on a beautiful, funny, whip-smart, Jewish girl I'll call Jody. Jody and I were both musicians, but she was far more accomplished than I. We were both homo sapiens too, but she was far more attractive than I. We became friends, nonetheless. Jody thought I was entertaining, if nothing else. I harbored what I thought was a well-hidden desire to do I-didn't-know-what with her. I had only the vaguest notions about the mechanics of physical intimacy, so my pining for her was long on intensity and short on specificity. It likely wasn't much of a secret either.

In fact, my father teased me mercilessly about Jody whenever he saw her around town.

"Woah, that Jody sure is lovely looking, isn't she? She's becoming a real Jewish American Princess. When are you going to ask her out on a date?"

Dear God, may the ground open up and swallow me whole. Right now. Amen.

The object of my obscure desire was chosen to be the music director and pianist for our high school's production of the musical *You're A Good Man, Charlie Brown*. I wanted to whoop with joy when she invited me to play bass for the show.

Rehearsals went along swimmingly until the moment Jody gathered our little pit band around the Steinway grand for a conference. She leaned over the piano to point out something in the score to the drummer and me. As she did so, her left breast smushed up against the back of my right hand, which was clutching the edge of the Steinway's lid. She lingered in that position for an eternity.

Should I snatch my hand away? Should I leave it there and hope she doesn't notice? I must have turned bright scarlet by the time Jody straightened up and released my hand.

"Was that there the whole time?" she asked, with an indecipherable look on her face.

"Yes," I stammered, wishing Scotty would beam me up.

"Oh," she said, playing her cards close to her chest. She reacted with neither disgust nor pleasure nor anger.

When I mentioned this incident to Jody many years later, she had no memory of it. That was a double whammy for me: I'd touched her breast—unintentionally, through her clothing, with the back of my hand. The shame and thrill of that moment was seared in my memory. But it apparently had made no lasting impression on her. I was glad Jody wasn't traumatized but I have to wonder if it was such a nothing incident because it was only lil' ole forgettable me who was the culprit.

After surviving the mortification of that moment, playing the show was a breeze. *You're A Good Man, Charlie Brown* was my first "pit" job. It wasn't jazz but I was glad to be the only bass player. What I played mattered—to the band, to the actors, and to the audience. It was intoxicating to be in the presence of my secret love for all those delicious hours. More than that, though, I felt simultaneously safe and seen as a musician for the first time. The bass part to "Suppertime," Snoopy's big number, is still in my fingers. Interpret that however you wish.

In the spring of junior year, our high school concert/marching band bussed down to Washington, DC, for the annual Cherry Blossom Festival parade. As the lone string bassist, I was relegated to the upstage left corner, adjacent to the low brass ghetto. My presence was superfluous. Whatever I played was obliterated by the firepower of trombones and tubas. But by that point, I was beyond caring. The concert band meant nothing to me; I was there for the hang.

After our arrival Friday night, a few of us hipsters-in-training, including my pals Korky and Ted, plus a guitarist named Bob, hosted a jam session in one of our hotel rooms. We wore ourselves out playing umpteen choruses of a blues in F and Stevie Winwood's "Glad."

I had blisters on my blisters by evening's end. It was worth it to feel hip, albeit temporarily.

The concert band performed in a competition the next night, then magically transformed into the mighty Tenafly High School Marching Band for the parade the following morning.

Since I played a non-mobile instrument, and since, being a teenager, I obviously couldn't be left to my own devices at the hotel, I tagged along as the band's unofficial documentarian. I'd brought along my trusty Bolex movie camera. I grabbed it and jumped on the bus with the rest of the gang.

In spite of the band director's persistent nagging, I'd managed to avoid getting roped into playing the sousaphone with the marching band, a fate that often befalls young bass players. Recall that I had recoiled at the "opportunity" to play a brass instrument a few years earlier. Also, I wasn't about to drag myself to school at seven a.m. for rehearsals or to show up for every dang football game. Not my jam, daddy-o. I had to admit, though, that there was something electrifying about the din of the band warming up and the buzz of the crowd gathering along the parade route. Having one foot in and one foot out struck the perfect balance.

After we had milled around for what must have been hours, the festivities finally got underway. The THS Marching Band executed its intricate footwork without misstep while simultaneously blasting song after song. I trotted alongside, shooting *cinéma vérité*–style footage of the drum majorettes, the woodwinds, the brass, and the glockenspiels. While I was lining up a wide shot of the trombones, someone grabbed me by my jacket sleeve.

"Lemme see your press pass."

It was a DC policeman.

"Press pass? I'm here with the band . . ."

"You have to have a press pass unless you're one of the performers."

"I'm a high school kid!"

"Step out of the street to the other side of the sawhorses."

My cheeks went hot; there was a whooshing in my ears. The cop pushed me toward the sidelines, then deposited me on the curb with a final dismissive shove. The band was fast marching out of sight.

I spun around, scanning the densely packed crowd for a familiar face. The cop was gone—back to patrolling for dangerous teens with loaded cameras, no doubt.

Concentrate, dammit! Where's the band? My legs were lead. I wanted to holler but had no voice. My innards burned with anger and panic.

I caught a glimpse of what I thought might be Allan the drum major's headdress plume rounding a corner. I bolted through the crowd on a diagonal, scorching a path through that jungle of humanity. Plunging ahead, I spied the familiar Tenafly Tiger stripes on a bass drum. There was Korky wailing away on his cornet and Ted honking on his sax. I doubled over, trying to quell my tears of relief.

Neither the band director, the chaperones, nor my friends knew what had transpired. I waited several days before spilling the beans to anyone, including my parents. Even though I knew I'd done nothing to deserve the rough treatment from that cop, I was terribly ashamed of the incident and how badly it had rattled me. During those frantic minutes, I thought for sure I'd be lost in the streets of DC forever. But I overcame the panic and found my way back to where I belonged.

Meeting Mrs. D.

1974

As a senior in high school, I had to decide which of my main pre-occupations—music, filmmaking, or broadcasting—to pursue before I could choose where to go to college.

I asked Mr. Bruno what he thought about my chances of becoming a professional musician

"I don't know, Billy," he said, scrunching up his caterpillar eyebrows. "It's a tough business. There's always work for bass players but there's lotsa guys out there too, vying for the same gigs."

"Did you go to music school?" I asked my teacher.

"Nah, I never went to college. My father taught me how to play the bass. I've been working since I was fourteen."

Mr. Bruno eventually wound up playing for Sinatra, so he must have been blessed with some serious talent.

My heart sank. I didn't have that kind of natural ability. I'd heard great bass playing, from Gary Karr, Paul Chambers, and Dave Holland, as well as my friend John Feeney from the BYO. My playing wasn't in the same universe. And the thought of having to audition to become a music major made my guts churn.

"I'm not saying don't do it," Mr. Bruno continued. "You're gonna have to up your game, though, if you wanna make it."

This conversation with Mr. B. was eerily similar to the ones I'd been carrying on piecemeal with my parents recently.

"We want you to do what makes you happy," my mother, ever the good cop, told me.

My father wasn't so sanguine.

"Sure, sure, but you have to be practical. I knew I wasn't going anywhere as a trumpet player; that's why I got my certificate from RCA."

That's the TV/radio repair course he took in the mid-1950s before going into business with his father. From what I could tell, his career choice fell rather short on the happiness dimension.

"Of course," my dad continued, "I had fun playing with your Uncle Zolly up in the Catskills."

"You guys are not helping," I told them.

If music is such an iffy proposition, isn't breaking into the movie business also a long shot? I'd made a handful of Super 8 mm films, but I knew that was small potatoes. A career in radio seemed far-fetched as well, since I had no clear goals and no actual on-air experience. This "yes, butting" from everybody was crazy-making.

Would someone please tell me what to do?

I couldn't have articulated this at seventeen, but I instinctively knew that making music my life's work would mean choosing to be visible and audible to people who would scrutinize my playing and, by association, me. Opting to study filmmaking would allow me to stay behind the scenes, protected from direct observation and judgment. I could be equally invisible behind a microphone.

Back to the old conundrum: Did I want to be in the light or the shadows? I got a charge out of playing bass in front of people; it also scared the bejeezus out of me.

While I was hacking my way through this jungle of confusion, my father arranged a meeting for me with an old friend who had graduated from Northwestern University, one of the schools I was considering.

Mrs. Devirgilio lived in an Upper East Side co-op. The building smelled like money. I rode the gilded elevator up to her floor and rang the doorbell.

The door swooshed open.

"Hello, Bill. I'm Mrs. Devirgilio."

There stood a tall, slender, silver-haired woman probably in her seventies, with long, neatly manicured fingers. She held her right hand out with her elbow tucked into her hip. I didn't know what the hell I was supposed to do.

"You should shake my hand," my new acquaintance admonished.

"Uh, yeah, sorry. Nice to meet you," I stammered.

Not the most auspicious start to our conversation.

Mrs. D.'s apartment was posh (there's simply no other word for it), with its plush carpeting, heavy burnished-wood furniture, and red velvet-papered walls adorned with abstract paintings. Her living room was dominated by a Steinway concert grand. There was a hush in the room that made me want to whisper.

"Tell me about you," the elegant woman asked.

"Well. I'm a pretty good student—mostly all As. I like to listen to jazz, and I jam with a couple of friends once a week or so."

"Who are your favorite musicians?"

"Oh, wow ... Mingus, Monk, Coltrane, Miles—"

"You have good taste. Are you familiar with a bassist named George Duvivier?"

Matter of fact, I was. George Duvivier was relatively unknown to the general public but well respected among his peers—a musician's musician.

"Uh huh, I'm pretty sure he's on an Eric Dolphy record I've heard," I ventured.

"Yes, *Out There*. George is a friend of mine. We play duets together sometimes. He's a wonderful man."

Mrs. D. plays with George Duvivier? Whoa. It took me a minute to absorb this information.

We chatted for a while longer, mostly about my interests. As a Northwestern alum, Mrs. D. asked what I might study if I went there. I told her I was considering majoring in film. She peered over her spectacles at me.

"You know, when you talk about music, your eyes light up in a way they don't when you talk about other things," she said. "You ought to keep that in mind."

My mind raced. Did my father suspect that Mrs. Devirgilio might try to persuade me to continue studying music? If so, did he think I had a chance to succeed? He lobbied for me to study something "practical," but I wondered if he secretly hoped I'd do something creative, an opportunity he had never allowed himself.

The only other school I was seriously considering was New York University, which reputedly had one of the best film programs in the country. Music, not so much. Northwestern, on the other hand, had a well-regarded radio, television, and film department as well as a top-notch music school.

My teenaged head was a hodgepodge of conflicting thoughts when I said goodbye to Mrs. D. (I remembered to shake her hand, though.) On the subway and bus rides back to Tenafly I thought: *No one's going to make this decision for you. You're gonna have to figure it out yourself.* I had a throbbing ache behind my eyes when I arrived home.

A few nights later, I lay sprawled on my bed, staring at my Beatles poster from the "White Album," trying to puzzle out the options.

Geez, I'm only seventeen. How the hell do I know what I'm going to be when I grow up? If I go to NYU that'll be the end of my bass studies—this seems certain. And do I really want to be in New York City, so close to my family?

At Northwestern, maybe I could be a radio/TV/film major and study bass with Warren Benfield, a teacher from the Chicago Symphony whose book, *The Art of Double Bass Playing*, I'd read and admired. That would be kind of a non-decision decision, a way to postpone making a definitive choice between music and film. And, as a bonus, I'd be in Evanston, Illinois, eight hundred miles from home.

I applied to NU and NYU and got accepted both places. The one-two-three punch of the benefits of Northwestern ultimately won the day. Attending the Creative Music Studio and my second summer at Lighthouse confirmed my desire to keep playing music—for the time being, anyway.

In late August 1974, I packed up Igor and my belongings and loaded everything into a borrowed Volkswagen Bus. With my mother in the driver's seat, I broadcast a silent farewell to my father and sister, Mr. Bruno, Korky, and my other friends. I left Tenafly with plenty of doubts but no regrets.

Finding Common Ground

1974–1976

Shortly after I arrived at Northwestern, things fell apart back home in New Jersey. My parents separated and my sister suffered what they used to call a nervous breakdown and had to be hospitalized. Without warning, my family hijacked center stage in my consciousness. I vowed to do whatever I could to reduce their stress. I'd make straight As, find a part-time job, and stay out of mischief. If I could just be perfect, I thought, things would surely be better at home.

Right.

College life hit me like a steamroller. Classes were onerous, with tons more reading and writing than I'd anticipated. Tests weren't multiple choice or fill-in-the-blank; they required clear thought and persuasive writing. As if that wasn't enough, so many diversions popped up to lure me away from academics: conflict with my mismatched roommate, a newly discovered taste for beer, and a cornucopia of attractive young women, one or two of whom intimated they might be interested in me. Then things became even more complicated—and music was the cause.

One evening during my first trimester, I was trundling down my dorm's corridor with Igor when a slender, scraggly bearded young man buttonholed me.

"Man, you're a bass player," he exclaimed, stating the obvious. "You play jazz, right?"

I nodded, wondering how he could tell what kind of music I played by my appearance.

"You ought to come to the jam session at Pike on Friday night."

"The what? Where?"

"Pi Kappa Alpha, man. It's a frat house on the north end of campus. There's a good drummer who lives there and a lot of happening musicians fall by every week."

"Um, yeah ... I'm new here. I don't know where any of the frats are ... and I don't have wheels."

"Don't worry about that. I'll pick you up. We're usually short of bass players. Meet me out front Friday around seven."

"OK. But who are you?"

"Oh, heh. My name's Wayne Willentz. I'm a film major. And I play jazz piano. Come on, you'll have a blast."

Hmm, film and jazz. My kind of guy.

"All right, Wayne. I'm Bill. I'll see you in a couple days."

That Friday, I drove with my new acquaintance to Pi Kappa Alpha, where I met a trio of musicians who would soon become my friends, bandmates, and mentors.

We came from disparate musical backgrounds. Wayne loved the Latin-tinged compositions of Chick Corea and Horace Silver. Ed Petersen, the tenor saxophonist, was a devotee of modernists John Coltrane and Wayne Shorter. The drummer, Jim Goodkind, came to jazz via rock and fusion; his favorite musicians were Tony Williams, who played with Miles Davis, and Stewart Copeland, the drummer for the Police. I was more interested than the others in avant-garde musicians like Art Ensemble of Chicago, Sam Rivers, and Eric Dolphy. This jumble of influences could have precipitated disaster when the four of us played together, but what resulted was a miraculous alchemy. Somehow, despite our stylistic differences, our quartet produced some powerful music.

Which was as troubling as it was wonderful. The band, which we called the Common Ground Quartet, began crowding out other responsibilities. I'd committed to being a model student (in my mind, anyway), but the music diverted my attention from the admittedly absurd standards I'd set for myself.

Rehearsing with CGQ exposed some deep holes in my fundamental knowledge of jazz. I discovered, for example, that I knew next to nothing about playing within the confines of song forms like the thirty-two-bar structure of hundreds of tunes from the Great American Songbook. Most of my experience playing non-orchestral music had been improvising without predetermined melody, meter, or harmonic structure, like the unfettered jamming I'd done with Korky. In that music, anything goes. Not so with the music of the CGQ.

Given our divergent musical preferences, Common Ground Quartet had an eclectic repertoire that included songs by Stevie Wonder, Thelonious Monk, Chick Corea, and Ornette Coleman, plus originals by Ed and Wayne. Those two guys were a few years older and already had fully formed musical personalities, while Jim and I were still in our larval stages. I was woefully unprepared to tackle most of this music.

"Bill, you're playing too busy," Wayne informed me at an early rehearsal. "This is a bossa nova. You gotta lay back on it."

"I'm not sure what you mean," I responded, trying to keep the defensiveness from my voice.

"Haven't you ever heard a Jobim record?"

"He's the guy who wrote 'Girl from Ipanema,' right?"

"Yeah, but there's more to it than knowing the name of a song he wrote. I'll lend you one of his LPs so you can check out what the rhythm section does."

Traditionally, jazz musicians learn how to play by absorbing the music of their predecessors. I hadn't done any of that work; I didn't even know I was supposed to do it. I hadn't studied jazz in a disciplined way, so I was lost trying to interpret chord symbols or play anything other than free or a 4/4 swing groove.

It's a testament to the patience of Wayne and Ed that they hung in there with Jim and me. I'd like to report that I responded diligently to their needling by stepping up my listening, studying, and practicing. I did a modicum of that, but I spent more energy faking my way through musical situations that were way beyond my capabilities. I don't know who my arrogant eighteen-year-old self thought he was fooling, but my bandmates were having none of it.

Once, in the middle of a bass solo, I heard Ed mutter, "Ah, exploring the dominant seventh chord," which was his unsubtle way of telling me I was sounding clumsy and foolish, which I'm sure I was. Another time I overheard this conversation between Ed and Wayne:

"When's he going to stop getting lost on these tunes?" Ed bemoaned.

"He'll get there. It's getting better, right?" Wayne replied.

"Yeah, but it's taking so damn long."

Ouch. I respected these guys and knew they were right. *(Remember the bowling alley, Harrison.)* I needed to get my shit together. I also had to go to classes, do the reading, write the papers, take the tests, and try to pass all my courses. Sometimes I felt like a bull fiddle coming apart at the seams.

Meanwhile, I was increasingly disappointed with the limitations imposed by the university. During an interview with an NU recruiter a year earlier, I'd been assured that I could study with Mr. Benfield, a promise that turned out to be either a mistake or a lie. Non-music majors were seldom permitted to study with "name" faculty, primarily because those teachers' schedules were usually full. In addition, the radio/TV/film department itself was a letdown. Students weren't allowed to take any practical classes or access any filmmaking equipment until junior year. Since I'd already made several films, I had arrived on campus champing at the bit to grab some 16 mm gear and get cracking. I resented being stymied on both fronts. Had I been aware of these two caveats during senior year of high school, I might have chosen NYU.

On the other hand, during most of my tenure at Northwestern, I was able to indulge my other youthful passion by working at WNUR, the campus radio station. Once or twice a week, beginning in early '75, I hauled an armload of LPs from my dorm room over to the dank basement of Swift Hall to do my four-hour shift as a jazz DJ.

WNUR had a decent, if somewhat scratched-up, collection of jazz records. I gleaned some tidbits of jazz history by pawing through the station's stacks and going "Hmm, what's this?" I found some oldies but goodies, such as two classic albums released the year I was born: *Ellington at Newport* and *Ella and Louis*, a recording of Ms. Fitzgerald and Mr. Armstrong singing duets with the Oscar Peterson Quartet. I also stubbed my musical toe on some clunkers, which shall remain nameless.

Broadcasting a radio show allowed me to develop and expand my musical taste. I chose the records I wanted to play; I decided what to say on the air. I could be whoever I wanted to be—a disembodied voice in the night, with the freedom to improvise anything, including a personality.

Still, my aggregate experience of Northwestern was discouraging. I thought about dropping out. If I did, then what? I was eight hundred miles from home, floundering with indecision. My parents had their own *mishigas* to manage. If I quit college, would I be a failure in their eyes? Would they be angry? One thing was certain: as my desire to play jazz increased, so did my dissatisfaction with the post–high school path I'd chosen.

The disaffection with Northwestern, the desire to prove to my bandmates that I could come up to their standards, the troubles at home; these were the ingredients of the stew I was roiling in as 1976 heated up. The conversation I'd had with Mrs. Devirgilio returned to my mind repeatedly as I tried to decide what to do about the intensifying distress.

Ed, Jim, Bill, and Wayne at Pi Kappa Alpha, 1975

Rites of Passage

1976–1977

I dropped out of Northwestern after the first trimester of my junior year, in which I'd flunked one course and taken an incomplete in another. Apparently, the handwriting was on the ivy-covered wall. My folks weren't thrilled with this decision but they were supportive enough to allow me to make my own mistakes. However, I was going to be on my own in every way, including financially.

I moved into a dreary but cheap second-floor walk-up in Evanston with my friends Kelly Sill (bass) and Dave Urban (trumpet), and secured a job at Laury's, a local record store. I took lessons with Mark Kraemer, a phenomenal Chicago Symphony Orchestra bassist who had famously won the CSO audition at the wee age of nineteen on a plywood bass, an unheard-of feat on both counts. Mark was the teacher who came up with the aphorism that became central to my relationship with my instrument of choice:

"You're never going to overpower the bass. You're going to have to outsmart it."

I practiced more than ever, which doesn't necessarily mean a lot or enough. I haunted jam sessions and accepted every gig I was offered, paid or not. I played with a revolving cast of aspiring (and perspiring) musicians at joints now long gone. We worked for pass-the-beer-stein tips. If the bar had an especially auspicious night the manager might slip us ten bucks apiece. The beer, praise Yahweh, was usually on the house.

After I withdrew from Northwestern, I felt it was time to upgrade to a better bass. This idea had been gestating ever since I'd had the chance to fool around with two high-quality instruments, John Feeney's and Dave Holland's. Although Kay made good double basses, they were constructed with plywood, a material that doesn't offer the resonance and complexity of tone available in instruments made with hardwoods like maple and spruce. Fingerboards on better basses are made of ebony instead of softer rosewood. These instruments are generically known as "carved," to distinguish them from plywood. Carved basses have better acoustic properties, which allow players to produce a more desirable sound more easily. They're also more expensive. Ease of operation was my biggest takeaway from having played those well-made carved basses. I lusted for one.

At the suggestion of my friend Kelly, I'd been taking Igor to a luthier named Laszlo Pinter for repairs. Mr. Pinter was sixtyish, Hungarian American, about my height, stocky, bespectacled, gray haired, and with a noticeably thick accent. Pinter's Violin Shop, at 3804 North Clark Street, was a place outside of time, dark and dusty, with the tang of wood glue, varnish, and paprikash hovering in the air. Though I first brought my bass there in 1975, the store wouldn't have been out of place in Dickens's era.

Mr. Pinter skittered around his shop like an animated gnome, fetching strings, cakes of rosin, violin chin rests, metronomes, and anything else his customers needed. He was a skilled craftsman who did excellent repair work on all grades and types of stringed instruments.

On one of my trips to Pinter's shop I casually mentioned that I might be in the market for a new bass. He lit up like a flare and insisted I follow him past his workbench to look at a few basses he had for sale. A newly built instrument from the Mittenwald region of Germany caught my eye. This bass was similar in size to my Kay, but was made mostly of maple with an ebony fingerboard. It played like butter, had a gleaming honey-colored finish, and a sweet tone to match.

"Meester Hareeson, you buy zees bass and you make zee very good beezness."

Mr. Pinter was as anxious to make a sale as I was to take that Mittenwald home. It took me a few visits and some fancy financial finagling, but in April of 1977 I bought that bass for $1,800. I also gave up my old frenemy Igor in trade as part of the deal. That was a huge chunk of change for me at the time but it was such an enormous leap upwards in sound quality and playability that I was sure

I'd struck gold. I began to understand how much impact a particular instrument can have on your playing.

On Wednesday, April 28, 1976, Wayne drove me downtown to 175 West Washington Street, home of the Chicago Federation of Musicians. I hefted my bass up a steep flight of stone stairs and into a voluminous rehearsal hall.

"Play something slow," intoned a grizzled old guy brandishing a clipboard. He looked as if he'd been hunched behind that card table since 1952.

I started on a C-major scale: C, D, E, F—

"OK, now play something fast."

Again I began a C-major scale, at a faster clip: C, D, E, F, G—

"Awright, you're in. That'll be eighty-two bucks now and another eighty next month."

And that was the sum total of my audition for Local 10-208. What the hell? Was this a joke? Maybe joining the union wasn't the career milestone I imagined.

April had already been a momentous month. Three weeks earlier, Ed had escorted me to Formal Resale Limited to purchase my first tuxedo, a shiny polyester number with outlandish wide lapels and frayed cuffs.

"This piece of junk is fine," Ed told me. "You don't want to spend a lot of dough on a work tux."

So I didn't. FRL had a fine selection of gleaming black shoes made of anything but leather as well as piles of "preworn" formal shirts. The salesman, whose name had to be Morty, sold me blue, beige, and white ruffled shirts as well as a set of cheap studs and cufflinks.

I wore that tux two nights later on a commercial gig led by Ed. It paid $58, which more than covered the cost of my new professional wardrobe.

Union card, check. Monkey suit, check.

Most of the music I'd previously dug fell by the wayside as I morphed into an insufferable jazz snob. No more Beatles, Santana, or CCR for me. I listened nonstop to Charlie Parker, Sonny Rollins, McCoy Tyner, Charles Mingus, Freddie Hubbard, Wayne Shorter, and many of the other post-1950s jazz masters. This exclusionary attitude may have kept the jazz fire stoked, but before long, I'd pay a steep price for my snooty single-mindedness.

I played commercial jobs here and there, usually with groups composed of my jazz cronies. We worked proms, weddings, and cocktail parties; the kind of gigs Chicago-area musicians refer to as "jobbing." On the East Coast they call these engagements "general business," which is such a lovely euphemism. Those jobs paid in the $50–$100 range, a small fortune in my hand-to-mouth world. My friends and I shared a repertoire and a similar disdain for this kind of work, which we judged was somehow beneath us. Of course it wasn't. But feeling superior was far easier to tolerate than feeling incompetent. *(Bowling alley, dude, bowling alley.)*

Though part of me knew I was as green as moldy mozzarella, my increasingly busy schedule gave me the unwarranted impression that I was on a surefire path to a successful career as a professional musician.

On the Road (Never) Again

1977–1978

The sweet Mittenwald bass hit the road with me later that year. Jim R., a keyboard player friend of mine, recommended me to Galen, the "star" of a touring lounge act. Jim pegged him as a "Liberace wannabe who wears spangled jumpsuits and plays a sparkling white baby grand piano." That didn't sound especially promising until I talked to the man himself.

"I can offer you a salary of two hundred and seventy-five dollars per week," Galen told me. "I usually give the guys a bump up after six months."

The ding-ding-ding of a Vegas one-armed bandit clanged in my brain. This was twice what my forty-hour-a-week job at the record store paid—and more than I'd ever earned doing anything.

How bad could it be? I said yes to the first road gig of my career.

Galen's band featured three keyboards, bass, and percussion. Once in a while the maestro would add violin to the mix, as if the arrangements weren't goopy enough. Galen's big show-stopping numbers were "MacArthur Park" and a *Jesus Christ Superstar* medley, both guaranteed to bring down the house. Or something like that. What the group lacked in funk we made up for in schmaltz.

Shortly after I joined, we spent two mind-numbing weeks each in Saginaw and Flint, Michigan. Then, in the dead of winter, we trekked to Wheeling, West Virginia, for a two-week stint at a supper club.

Without traffic and under good road conditions, the drive from Chicago to Wheeling is a hefty eight hours. Galen and his partner Dale (the band's percussionist) drove there in the former's Cadillac. It wasn't pink, but it might as well have been. The second keyboardist, Michael, drove with his girlfriend. Jim and I drew the short straw and were tasked with transporting the band's equipment and ourselves in a twenty-foot-long U-Haul truck.

We loaded the U-Haul at Galen's suburban home late in the afternoon, hoping to get to Wheeling by midnight. This band had a shit-ton of gear. We carried Galen's Yamaha grand piano and a Hammond B-3 organ with two enormous Leslie speakers, which looked like twin Victorian armoires with spinning horns in place of their top drawers. We also schlepped a Fender Rhodes stage model keyboard, Mini-Moog, Polymoog, and Mellotron synthesizers, a full drum kit that included a large gong and a set of orchestra bells, my double bass and bass guitar, an unwieldy PA system, instrument amplifiers, and ancillary junk (cables, lights, fancy music stands, and the band's music library).

It was a frigid and snowy evening. Jim and I blasted the U-Haul cab's heater all the way across Illinois and Indiana. At some God-forsaken point west of Columbus, Ohio, on I-70 at about eleven p.m., our truck conked out and wouldn't reignite no matter what tricks we tried. The gas tank was half full. The bastard just up and died in the middle of nowhere. From the looks of it, that particular truck was ready to collect social security to begin with, so it's possible that the timing belt broke or something equally calamitous happened. I don't believe we ever got a diagnosis.

What we did get was the "opportunity" to remove all the equipment from that U-Haul and reload it onto a replacement truck the company sent ninety minutes later. It was a fucking nightmare.

Jim and I got rolling again long past midnight, temperatures in the single digits, snow drifts and ice patches lurking like landmines everywhere. We were a couple of half-frozen twenty-three-year-olds, punch-drunk with exhaustion, trying to pilot this behemoth through unknown territory. Somehow, I made an egregious navigation error in the wee hours. As near as I can figure, we took the wrong fork at the junction of I-70 and I-77 and wound up heading south instead of continuing west. In those pre-GPS days, it was all too easy to veer off track and not realize it for several hours, which is exactly what happened.

The rising sun was making me squint as I steered our U-Haul through the tiny village of Palestine, West Virginia (population eight hundred), at around seven a.m. We'd finally gotten wise to our ruinous wrong turn and were trying to claw our way back to northbound

I-77. We crept along at maybe twenty-five miles an hour down a local two-lane road when I passed a school bus pulled over on our right. Before the retinal image of the bus registered in my over-tired brain, a local cop was on our tail, siren a-blaring and lights a-flashing.

"License and registration," demanded the officer, all business behind his drugstore wraparounds. "Y'all passed a school bus. That's a moving violation."

I tried to reason with him.

"Look, officer, we're from Chicago. We've been driving all night and got lost on our way to Wheeling. Where we come from, school buses have flashing red lights and a stop sign that sticks out from the side of the bus when they're loading passengers. I didn't even see the bus."

This cop wasn't having any of my city slicker guff. He confiscated my driver's license and shoved a summons into my unwilling hands. He ordered me to follow him to the Wirt County Courthouse, where, in a couple of hours, I could literally "tell it to the judge."

Jim and I were freaking out—drowsily. All I wanted was to go to sleep and magically wake up after all the gear was set up onstage at the club in Wheeling. There wasn't a damn thing we could do except sit there waiting for the courthouse to open. I was delirious with anxious questions:

Were they going to throw me in the slammer? Was there going to be some exorbitant fine I couldn't afford to pay? Would we make it to the gig? How furious was Galen going to be?

At nine a.m. sharp we were hustled into the courtroom. The judge (played by Rod Steiger in *In the Heat of the Night*) had no sympathy for my sob story. Jim and I scraped together enough cash to pay the fine. I was given a stern talking-to, and my license was reluctantly returned. We called Galen to let him know what was happening. He was incredulous. And pissed that we were going to be arriving so late, assuming we didn't get lost again.

We dragged ourselves back to the truck. Jim mercifully took the wheel, and we rolled into Wheeling around midday. Mike and Dale helped us unload the U-Haul. We set the equipment up, did a quick sound check, and crashed hard at the nearby motel for a few hours before showtime.

After a few months with Galen & Co. I had my answer to the naïve question I'd flippantly posed when I took the gig: How bad could it be? Pretty damn bad.

Night after night, the dreck we played spread throughout the venue like a thick, somnambulant fog. There was no groove, no energy, nothing I could hang on to. Worst of all, I couldn't do anything to make it better. My frustration echoed what I imagined pumping coins into those one-armed bandits without ever hitting the jackpot must feel like to a gambler.

Not long after the Wheeling trip, my relationship with Galen came to the abrupt end of its road. The specifics are hazy, but I believe he'd hired me for several weeks of work, which fell through too late for me to try to book other work. This infuriated me. I was counting on that income and thought Galen owed me some compensation for losing those bookings. He did not agree.

So, like the mature, reasonable person I was then, I fumed silently, then canceled a date he'd booked me on with a scant few days' notice. I felt vindicated. Galen was livid. When I explained that I'd simply done to him what he'd done to me, he hissed, "I don't owe you a fuckin' thing," and slammed down the phone.

I filed a complaint with the Chicago Federation of Musicians for what I considered to be a breach of our verbal agreement.

My final sighting of Galen was in front of the union's trial board, where both of us were admonished to, essentially, stop being assholes. No compensation was awarded.

In retrospect, there's no doubt in my mind that Galen should have offered the guys in the band some token amount to make up for the canceled work. But I'm embarrassed to have responded to a wrong with another wrong. I could have quit sooner. It was pigheaded and unprofessional of me to leave Galen and the band hanging like that.

A scant couple of years earlier I'd envisioned life traveling with a great jazz group as the ideal way to live. My wretched experience with Galen cured me of any romantic notions I'd ever had about that life-style. Aside from the occasional one-nighter here and there, I never hit the road again.

Part II

Mr. B. and Me

1979–1981

I'm leaning against the wall outside Warren Benfield's studio after transporting myself and my bass up to the second floor of DePaul University's music building. There's a bead of sweat oozing down my right temple. I've been chasing after this man for years. I read his book in high school; he was half the reason I decided to attend Northwestern five years ago. I've finally caught up with him.

I hear someone on the other side of the door, a fellow student maybe, playing an unrecognizable passage on a double bass. There's murmuring, then a repeat of the same passage. Laughter. More conversation, which is too faint to make out.

The door swings open. Out strides a smiling, energetic young man, cradling the neck of his encased bass in the crook of his left arm.

"Hey, so you're the new guy?" he says, right hand outstretched.

"Yeah, I guess so," I say, squeezing his hand.

"John Floeter."

"Hi, John. Bill Harrison."

"Hey, Bill. Have fun with Mr. B. I'll see you around like a doughnut." And off he goes, wheeling his bass down the corridor.

I gotta get me one of them bass wheels.

I pick up my instrument and enter the room, my heart slapping against my ribs like a rockabilly bass solo.

"Hello!" bellows the man sitting behind a large oak desk. "I'm Warren Benfield."

I'd know him anywhere. He looks exactly like the photos in his book: receding slate-gray hair, black-rimmed Walter Cronkite glasses, three-piece navy suit, affable grin.

"Unpack your bass and let's get going," says Mr. B.

And off we go.

During my two years working at Laury's Records and that brief but memorable interlude with Galen, I'd heard that Warren Benfield had become the primary bass instructor at DePaul University. I started to wonder what it might be like to finish my bachelor's degree there, this time as a music major. Returning to college certainly pleased my parents, whose unspoken anxiety about my "future" radiated through the phone whenever I spoke to one of them. I wasn't gung-ho about the idea but I applied to DePaul, got accepted, and began taking classes there in the fall of 1979. I'd wanted to study with Mr. Benfield for a long while, so this was my shot.

Mr. B. had been appointed to the Chicago Symphony Orchestra by music director Rafael Kubelik in 1949. He was fired when the maestro left, rehired by Fritz Reiner, and then retired in 1987, near the end of Sir Georg Solti's reign. Benfield had been a student of Anton Torello, principal bassist with the Philadelphia Orchestra for over forty years, and the first bass instructor at Curtis Institute of Music. I mention these biographical details because I was so intimidated by Mr. B.'s musical pedigree as well as by the long list of fine bass players who'd come through his studio. They included jazz musicians Rufus Reid and Steve Rodby, virtuoso soloists Gary Karr(!) and Jeff Bradetich, plus many successful orchestral bassists, like Edwin Barker, principal bass of the Boston Symphony Orchestra.

Mr. B. tried to allay my fears.

"Forget about all that," he advised. "Right now, you're the most important person in the world to me."

It was a kind gesture. I never bought it.

Benfield was "old school" in so many ways: the dapper suits (which I imagined he wore even when sleeping), the hearty we're-all-in-this-together attitude, and, especially, his teaching style. He'd learned to read and play music using *solfege*, a dated system of assigning syllables to each step of a scale. Remember "Do-Re-Mi" from *The Sound of Music*? That's *solfege*. There's nothing inherently wrong with the system itself, but it wasn't much use to me at that particular time. I had a profusion of technical, hands-on-the-bass catching up to do. *Solfege* couldn't address those issues.

Early in my studies with Mr. B., I happened to be on the phone with my mother one day. I told her Mr. Benfield was teaching me *solfege.* There was a long pause on the other end of the line, then she asked me,

"What does selling fish have to do with playing the bass?"

It was more relevant a question than she knew.

Some of Benfield's colleagues thought him a bit of a dinosaur, both as a player and as a teacher. He had an encyclopedic knowledge of the orchestral literature. But his abundant natural ability plus his decades of on-the-job experience created a barrier between us. I'm not sure if it was more Mr. B. or me, but I had difficulty making progress with the basics of physical technique while I studied with him. This became evident, for example, when I tried to learn the fiendishly difficult bass part to "Ein Heldenleben," Richard Strauss's tone poem.

"Let me correct those fingerings and bowings for you," suggested Mr. B.

"But . . . you gave me these last week," I reminded him.

"Oh, right. Well, let's try it another way."

"OK, but how should I practice them?"

"Well, that's technical [pronounced "teshnical"]. Go home and work it out."

Apparently, this figure-it-out-for-yourself method was Torello's, along with the quirky pronunciation of "technical." As much as I appreciated the humor, I found the lack of specific guidance frustrating.

Whenever I hadn't practiced adequately for that week's lesson (alas, a far-too-common occurrence that had been my m.o. since my days with Mr. Roviaro), I tried to induce Mr. B. to tell me one of his many stories. One or two of them could easily eat up most of the hour, which meant I could avoid embarrassing myself with my lack of preparedness.

When I had practiced sufficiently, I was able to glean some useful advice from Mr. B. about phrasing, articulation, sound production, and dynamics. I incorporated some of his tips into my practice routine, such as the suggestion to work out two different sets of fingerings for a particular passage, then sleep on it.

"The best fingering will emerge the next time you practice," he'd say.

He was right more often than not.

Mr. B.'s emphasis on musicality, combined with the lack of direction regarding technique, forced me to find my own solutions. His teaching style fostered creative self-reliance but also led to some poor habits I had to correct later in my career, when it was more challenging to do so.

Notwithstanding all of that, Benfield's unflagging encouragement helped me tremendously. His enthusiasm, deep knowledge for his beloved orchestral repertoire, and charm propelled me forward as a musician and as a man. He planted the seed of real confidence that (slowly, painfully) supplanted the bogus self-importance I'd often used as a shield to hide my incompetence.

Two-Bass Hit

1980

I found my next two basses while I was studying with Mr. B. at DePaul. The first was an early-twentieth-century instrument imported by the Czech violin maker and string merchant Janek Juzek. This bass was huge. It had a dark chocolate finish, violin corners, and a round back. I bought it because I wanted a bigger sound than the Mittenwald could produce. The burly Juzek gave me that boost in volume, but the trade-off was an uncomfortable increase in string length (or, if you want to get teshnical, *mensure*).

The Czech bass's string length, measured from the bridge to the nut (the horizontal strip of ebony at the top of the fingerboard), was a good two inches longer than the Mittenwald's—long enough to make the lowest positions too wide for my fully outstretched south paw. Sad to say, it took me four painful, frustrating years to figure out that the Juzek was not the right bass for me. At the time, I couldn't understand why I was having so much trouble playing that thing in tune. *I must not be practicing enough*, I thought. And, since my practice regimen had never been especially consistent, I had reason to think that putting in more time would solve the problem.

Only, it didn't. The chronic soreness in my left hand should have given me a clue that something was awry. I blamed these difficulties on myself, rather than considering the possibility that the Juzek was simply too big for me. This lack of self-awareness combined with my usual stubbornness was a variation on the hubris theme, a sort of macho "I can make this work" by force of will.

Meanwhile, I compounded my difficulties by purchasing yet another bass, a tall, slender, blonde Götz, which had an even longer *mensure*. I bought this giraffe-like bass because its spit-fire *pizzicato* attack was so much better for jazz than the Juzek, which had a slow response time and a darker sound.

I should have heeded my mother's advice about blondes, because the Götz proved to be way too much for me to handle. I played both basses for my senior recital, which, from my present vantage point, was insane. So much for outsmarting the bass.

Peter and the Wolf[1]

1981

n January 1981 I received the following life-changing phone call:

"Hi, is this Bill?"

"Uh huh, that's me."

"Hey, Bill. This is Peter Polzak. We met at Collette's a while back."

"Um, OK." I had no memory of meeting anyone by that name at that bar, but I thought I'd play along.

"I was wondering if you'd be interested in playing a night with my trio at the Pump Room? I'm looking for a new bass player."

Now he had my full attention. I'd heard there was a jazz trio playing at that club in the swanky Ambassador East Hotel. Of course I was interested.

"Can you make it this Friday? The gig is eight to twelve and pays sixty-two fifty. The only downside is that you have to wear a tuxedo. Oh, and the parking sucks around there."

That was pretty good bread and, by this time, wearing a tux was no longer a big deal.

"Sure, Peter. Sounds good. I'll see you then."

I later learned that Peter was looking for someone to replace Greg Mitchell, who had been the bassist in his trio until his recent tragic death. According to my friend and colleague Bob Sutter, Greg died of cardiac arrest one night in between a rehearsal and a show with singer/actress Diahann Carroll. Bob, Greg, and a few other musicians were having dinner, laughing and telling gig stories, as musicians are wont to do. Greg, an asthmatic like Bob (and me), went into a coughing fit at the table and was having a tough time breathing. The two of them repaired to the men's room, where Bob attempted to help Greg

---

1   Velvel is my Yiddish name; it means "wolf."

recover. Sadly, his efforts, as well as those of the EMTs who answered the 911 call, failed.

Not only had Greg played bass with Peter, they'd also been the closest of friends—so much so that Peter named his son after his bassist. I wasn't hip to any of these details when I donned my least-ragged tuxedo and found my way to the Pump Room on January 9. All I knew was that I was auditioning for a steady jazz gig.

A self-described "blue-collar jazz piano player," Peter grew up behind the Cheddar Curtain in Green Bay, where the natives' spiritual lives revolve around their beloved Packers. A mesomorph about my height (five eight), Peter was a white guy who came from a large Catholic family with Bohemian roots. The family traced its bloodline back to the Ringling family of circus fame. Show business was in his DNA.

Peter's introduction to jazz couldn't have been more different than mine. One of his older brothers played him a Dave Brubeck album, which made a huge impression on the young pianist. I thought Brubeck was square as hell, one of the many white guys who weren't doing much more than popularizing jazz for white audiences. Peter also got hooked on the music of Vince Guaraldi. The latter's *Charlie Brown's Christmas* LP was cool, but I hardly thought of Guaraldi as a heavy jazz player.

I didn't change my mind about either of those pianists (though I came to enjoy playing some of their compositions), but Peter and I agreed about another prominent pianist, Bill Evans. Evans played an essential role on Miles Davis's *Kind of Blue*, one of the first jazz records that caught my ears way back in Korky's bedroom. He's best known for his piano/bass/drums trios, in which he developed a looser, more spontaneous and democratic way of approaching the music.

Peter's playing was steeped in Evans's multilayered harmonic palette. I'd not yet encountered anyone who used this language as proficiently as he. Right away I knew I could learn a lot about this style of playing if I got a chance to hang out with Peter for a while. Plus, I needed a regular gig.

I don't know how many bass players Peter auditioned for the job, but for unknown reasons, he hired me for the Pump Room gig. Our differences in musical and geographic origins didn't prevent us from hitting it off well, on and off the bandstand. In addition to his obvious musical talent, Peter was an easy-going guy with a crackling sense of humor. No one could ever replace Greg, of course, but over time, Peter and I became close friends. Our musical association would last for many years to come.

The Daley School of Jazz

Now, I'm *not* saying I didn't learn plenty during my time as a music major at DePaul University.

Music historian Dr. Brown taught me I should never again register for a lecture class scheduled for nine a.m. His was a snooze fest, except for the presence of my friend Mona, a talented, knock-down gorgeous flutist. We sat close together in the back row, which somehow gave Dr. Brown the impression that we were lovers. We weren't, but I let him continue to think we were because it seemed to drive him insane with jealousy. He was at least twice our age, bald, frumpy, and married, so I don't know what the hell he was thinking. And, it's possible that Mona and I flirted a teensy bit.

I also discovered that classical music history was not my bag, especially first thing in the morning after working until one a.m. the previous night. Mona and I made a pact to take notes for one another on the days one of us didn't make it to class, a common occurrence.

On the other hand, Ray Wilding-White's Musicianship 101 classes were oddly entertaining. He was the quintessential absent-minded professor, who dressed like a hobo and chewed his tongue incessantly. Wilding-White sometimes said wildly inappropriate things to a classroom full of eighteen-year-old music nerds. I recall a moment when, apropos of nothing, he used the phrase "twenty minutes of fellatio," inciting several moments of uncomfortable chair shuffling and furtive eye rolling.

Wilding-White also had a formidable intellect and an illustrious history in academia and media. He had earned degrees from Juilliard, the New England Conservatory, and Boston University. He had worked on air at radio stations WGBH (where he was awarded a Peabody) and WFMT. He penned numerous compositions, many influenced by Charles Ives and John Cage. Wilding-White was a pioneer of electronic music and an avid art photographer.

He was also a mess of a man who, for reasons only known to him, wanted to be my pal. I was a few years older than most of the other students and already a working professional musician, so perhaps that gave him the mistaken impression that we were somehow peers. We'd occasionally meet for lunch at a local joint with a Tolkien-inspired menu. (Bilbo Burger, anyone?) During one of those lunch dates, Wilding-White bellyached to me about his problems with women.

"My wife told me she's leaving me," he said.

"Geez, Ray, that's terrible."

"Yeah, and my girlfriend broke up with me too."

"Uh ..."

"Yeah, I lost 'em both on the same day."

It pains me to admit that I did little to discourage this inappropriate familiarity. I called Wilding-White "Ray" in class, as if we were buddies instead of professor and undergraduate. I made "casual" references to gigs I was doing or venues I'd played, which had to be annoying to some of my classmates. In short, I acted like a pompous ass. I wish I could have a do-over on this episode of my life.

By contrast to Brown and Wilding-White, I loved Kurt Westerberg's ear-training sequence without reservations. Westerberg was a genuinely decent guy, younger and hipper than most of the faculty. After a semester working with melodies and harmonies derived from major and minor scales, he told us it was "time to cleanse our ears of tonality," by which he meant that we needed to integrate more chromatic sounds into our aural skill sets.

A favorite moment from his class happened during an exercise we did periodically. Westerberg would play three notes on the piano for each student, who then had to identify the two musical intervals (or distances) between the notes. One day, when it was my turn, he played an ascending minor third followed by an ascending perfect fifth. These happen to be the first three notes of the Carpenters' classic "Close to You," corresponding to the lyrics "Why do birds ..." Instead of providing the answer, I sang the notes to the rest of the line. It brought the house down. Thank you very much, I'll be here all semester.

What I *am* saying is that my real education during my DePaul years occurred on Monday nights at a jazz club called Orphans, up the street from DePaul, under the guiding influence of saxophonist Joe Daley.

The front section of Orphans was a nondescript bar. The back room had a stage, a mostly operational grand piano, stage lights, a sound system, the whole shebang. I hung out back there many nights, performing or listening. Orphans is where I met two of my favorite women, each of whom became my girlfriend for a minute—though not simultaneously. It's also where I heard and met some remarkable musicians during my earliest days in Chicago.

Jazz musicians comprise a notably peculiar subculture. Quirkiness is one of the most valued personality traits; the more eccentric you are, it seems, the more you're likely to be thought cool. No one I knew embodied this kind of idiosyncrasy better than Joe.

Daley was a stone bebopper in the 1950s. Though his playing had evolved since then, he still spoke in what I call "terse hipsterese," a patois from that period in which "hey" could be an entire conversation. He's the only guy I ever heard use the 1940s-era term "geeters" to mean money, as in "Lemme go get the geeters from that shyster club owner."

Joe was one of the few players of his era in Chicago who embraced some of the musical innovations of John Coltrane and Ornette Coleman. He had remarkable technical command of the tenor saxophone and became one of the most sought-after teachers in the Midwest by the time he was in his forties.

When I met him, Joe was sixtyish, still baby-faced and handsome, with an enviable head of jet-black hair. He eschewed wearing a tuxedo on formal gigs.

"They bug me," he'd say with a grimace.

Joe was famous for being brusque. Former sax students tell horror stories of getting sent home early from lessons, after paying the full fee, of course, if they hadn't practiced to his satisfaction.

"Come back when you can play it," he'd growl.

One night, a drummer Joe felt wasn't up to snuff was sitting in. Daley stopped the band in the middle of the tune and banished the guy from the bandstand with a curt "Not makin' it, babe."

Around 1980, I heard through the jazz grapevine that Kelly Sill, one of Chicago's premier bassists, was leaving Joe's group. Whoever inherited that job would have huge shoes to fill. John Campbell, a legendary pianist who was in Joe's band at the time, called to ask me if I'd consider taking over the bass stool. Why, yes. Yes, I would.

Having heard the stories of Joe's bluntness, however, I was jittery the night I sat in with the band for my "audition." John had advised me to "play your ass off like you always do," which was supportive but did little to diminish my fears. I'd listened to the band many times before that night, so I was familiar with Joe's repertoire.

When he called Benny Golson's complex tune "Stablemates" for our first number together, I was ready. During my solo chorus, after he and John had already taken their swings at the chord changes, Joe indicated with a brief smile and a subtle nod that I was *in*.

Joe was always teaching, even when he wasn't. The values he communicated included virtuosic mastery of one's instrument, relying on one's ears, having equal fluency in all twelve keys, being as expressive as possible, and playing with a good time feel (i.e., swinging). When he liked what you were doing, he'd let you know with a word or two at most. I gathered from my saxophone-playing friends who'd studied with Joe that he was more forthcoming with criticism when he thought they were doggin' it.

Once, I executed some tricky phrase during a solo, to which Joe immediately responded, "Chops!" Another time, in the midst of one of our weekly excursions into free group improvisation, something I played elicited an appreciative "Ears!" I suppose I'd learned a thing or two since my Common Ground Quartet days.

Joe may have been parsimonious with praise, but his exemplary playing and high artistic standards, evident even when we were performing just for Claudia, the cocktail waitress, motivated me to work hard and stay focused on my musical goals—really for the first time.

Playing with Joe and the musicians he invited to the bandstand was a privilege. In addition to John Campbell and drummer Joel Spencer, I had the good fortune to perform with some of the most inspiring musicians I've ever heard, including drummers Rusty Jones and Paul Wertico as well as pianists Bobby Schiff and Larry Luchowski. Joe's gigs reinforced the principle that your level of ability rises when you're surrounded by more accomplished musicians. There's something supernaturally satisfying about connecting musically with simpatico musicians. Some nights I believe I played better with Joe's band than I ever did throughout the remainder of my career.

After about a year of Mondays at Orphans, I became romantically entangled with one of the aforementioned women. She was a talented bass player who was attending the University of Illinois at Urbana-Champaign. I'd often drive the two and a half hours downstate to hang out with her after my Saturday-night gig.

Sometimes it was difficult to tear myself away early enough on Monday to make Joe's gig. On several occasions I sent a sub to Orphans. When that happened too often, Joe replaced me with another bassist who was willing to show up consistently. I was angry about this at the time, but I now know he was right. I chose pleasure over my commitment to his band; a forgivable sin, perhaps, but one I regret. Part of me thought I'd learned all I was going to learn from Joe by then, which was both cavalier and untrue. I'd like a do-over on that one too, please.

I learned some useful stuff at DePaul. And they gave me that piece of paper showing I'd done all the schoolwork needed to earn a bachelor's degree. But the Daley School of Jazz was where I launched into the real world of the music that mattered most to me.

Miss Golub and the Chopin Liszt

1982

I handed Miss Golub an oblong slip of paper with the words "Chopin Liszt" printed along the top edge. She glanced at it for a moment, then looked up at me quizzically.

"What is this?"

"It's a shoppin' list," I said, realizing in that instant what an idiotic mistake I'd just made.

"Oh."

"My mother sent it to me. As a joke."

Miss Golub stared at me with a mixture of pity and disappointment.

"Why don't we get started?" she said, patting the piano bench next to her.

I gingerly placed my copy of Bach's "Two-Part Inventions" on her Steinway's music rack and managed to sit down without tripping over my own feet.

Goldie Golub (1909–2000) was a slight yet formidable presence. All of five foot nothing and ninety pounds, she was in her midseventies when I began studying with her at Roosevelt University early in the '80s.

I was a rank beginner when I met Miss Golub. My preadolescent forays into playing the accordion accounted for almost nothing, technique-wise. The physical touch of the squeezebox's keyboard is kid stuff compared to the macho demands of a grand piano. And pushing chord buttons did little to develop any piano-worthy strength in my left hand.

"You have about one and a half fingers," Miss Golub told me at my first lesson. "You're going to need all ten if you want to play the piano."

I smiled, assuming this was a bit of pedagogical hyperbole. She did not. And it was not. Miss Golub, who came from an era long before the honorific Ms. became normalized, worked at a finer level of technical detail than any of my previous teachers. There was no faking it in her studio; you either played the exercise with absolute precision or you took the same material home for another week—or for as long as it took to get it right. Her patient, serious demeanor induced me to practice diligently for the first time in my life. It was a matter of respect. She made me want to work hard—not to please her but to fulfill my own sense of integrity, intermittent though it was.

Miss Golub and her family had escaped Russian pogroms when she was five. She spent her childhood in Chicago's Austin neighborhood, then a primarily Jewish enclave. Young Goldie took advantage of one of the few luxuries her working-class family could afford—a piano. She had to work for a few years after graduating from Marshall High School before she was able to pursue further musical studies. She eventually earned bachelor's and master's degrees from Roosevelt, then taught hundreds of students there until she retired at the age of eighty-nine.

I pulled the silly "Chopin Liszt" prank early in our working relationship, before I grasped the depth of Miss Golub's commitment to both the music and to me. I don't doubt that she had a sense of humor, but music wasn't a game to her. It was her lifelong passion and she wasn't about to allow her students to accord it any less gravitas than she did.

I had little ability at the piano; that much I knew. I now believe that my foolhardy attempt at comedy was my way of trying to connect with her, to distinguish myself from among her coterie of truly talented students.

Forty years later, it's obvious to me that the only acceptable way to earn Ms. Golub's respect was to work persistently at the craft. I never became a pianist per se, but her meticulous approach to music infused my subsequent practice with a renewed level of attention to fundamentals like intonation, articulation, and dynamics. My studies with her were, I now see, the third leg of the proverbial three-legged stool of my music education—the other two being the teachings I was fortunate to receive from Joe Daley and from Peter.

Miss Golub was the brilliant piano teacher who helped me become a better bass player.

I'll Have the Square Fish

April 6, 1981

I'm wrenched from sleep at around five a.m. by something gouging out my guts with a bayonet. I try shifting positions but can't find one that eases the scraping sensation a few inches southwest of my navel. I stare at my nightstand clock, loath to breathe for fear of exacerbating whatever the hell this is. *Did I eat something rotten at yesterday's brunch? Is this some demonic flatulence?*

At 6:05, desperate, I call Ruth, my ex-girlfriend. She's likely on her way to work as a radiology resident at Saint Francis Hospital in Evanston. I'm the last person she'd expect to hear from, especially at this hour. I skip the pleasantries and describe my symptoms to her.

"I don't know what it is," Ruth tells me. "But you ought to get yourself to an ER. Don't wait."

I'd never been a patient in a hospital; the thought of it scares the bejeezus out of me.

"Can I come to Saint Francis?"

I trust that I'll get the straight dope from Dr. Ruth and her colleagues.

"Uh, OK. Come in through the ER and have them page me."

Next, I ring my current girlfriend, Lindy, who immediately offers to drive me up to Evanston. I throw on yesterday's clothes and hobble down two long flights of stairs bent over like a ninety-year-old.

At the hospital I'm hustled into an exam room. Ruth materializes with another doctor, who asks me a few questions and palpates my abdomen. I fight the urge to punch him in the kidneys.

"We're going to get some X-rays to make sure, but I'm ninety-five percent positive you're going to need an emergency appendectomy."

My heart gallops toward my suddenly arid throat.

"You should call whoever you want to notify now. We'll probably take you right from radiology to the OR."

I feel like throwing up on this guy's shoes.

My mother grabs the phone on the seventh ring. She had one foot out the door of her Bergenfield, New Jersey, garden apartment when I dialed her number. I explain what's happening and assure her I'll call as soon as possible after the surgery.

Ruth returns to the radiology department about fifteen minutes after my photo shoot, brandishing a fistful of X-rays. She's practically beaming.

"You have a classic case of appendicitis. These images are going into our department's teaching file."

Fan-fucking-tastic.

I guess our breakup hadn't been as contentious as I remembered. Either that or she's conspiring to have me dispatched on the operating table. Moments later somebody jams an IV into my left forearm as a man in a long white coat leans over my gurney.

"You have anesthesia," is what I hear him say.

"NO! I haven't had any anesthesia yet."

He smiles with just a hint of condescension.

"I'm the anesthesiologist. I'll be giving you the medication in your IV."

"Uh, right." *Stupid me.*

I'm out before we rumble to the elevator.

Did they do the surgery? Because, damn, some bastard is skewering me in the belly with a bowie knife, over and over.

I want to call out to see if anyone is within earshot but I can't make my mouth work. I need some pain meds, stat. A woman in a light blue outfit floats into my field of vision and asks how I'm doing.

"I'm in a lot of fucking pain," I say, but it comes out as "Ffffmmmmmphth."

"I know you're uncomfortable, Mr. Harrison, but we have to make sure you're fully clear of the anesthesia before we can give you anything for the pain."

She disappears. I retreat into my chasm of misery. Dark thoughts swirl through my addled mind: *Will this pain ever stop? How long will*

I be in here? When will I be able to play my bass? Wait—when will I be able to walk or climb stairs? What about school? How will I make a living? Holy shit.

After half an eternity, I'm bounced awake as my gurney *thunks* through a set of double doors. I'm being wheeled through a garish florescent-lit hallway. Each bump feels like we're driving over one of Chicago's infamous potholes in a rickshaw.

Two meaty orderlies dump me like a side of beef onto my hospital bed. Then the blue lady (she must be a nurse) appears and fusses with the IV bag swinging from a pole on my right.

Whoa. What did you give me? I ask with my eyebrows.

Nurse Blue flashes me a Cheshire Cat grin.

"Oh . . . that's Demerol. Pretty great, right?"

The pain melts like whipped butter on a just-toasted English muffin.

Good God. This is what heroin must be like. Yeah baby, let's hang out here for, like, the next few years. That'd be peachy.

I descend into a narcotized slumber.

A party is happening in my room—one I haven't been invited to. Hold on—is that my mother chatting with Lindy? Is that Ruth telling Mom the surgery "went without a hitch and he's now minus one diseased appendix"?

I make a guttural noise. The group flocks over to me, cooing like turtle doves. I hold back tears at the sight of my mother, who must have hopped on the first flight out of Newark to get here so soon. She, Lindy, Ruth, my friends Bruce and Dave—all huddle around the bed and barrage me with questions I can't answer. Words still refuse to travel from my brain to my mouth. Mom asks if I want to suck on some ice chips, which suddenly sounds like the most delicious suggestion ever made. I nod. Lindy holds a Styrofoam cup to my mouth (Is it really *my* mouth?) and I slurp a couple of cold, wet discs.

And that's all I remember of that first day. The rest is wiped clean, due, I imagine, to a combination of the aftereffects of the anesthesia, the blissful loveliness of the Demerol, and the erosion of time.

By Tuesday I'd regained the power of speech and could communicate with my visitors as well as the parade of medical personnel that descended on me like a committee of vultures. Appendectomies performed at that time were considered major surgery, because doctors had to make a six-inch incision through the abdominal wall. I missed the opportunity for a laparoscopic appendectomy, which would have been far less invasive. They were first performed experimentally in 1983. Oh well.

As a result, I found out that laughing is the worst thing you can do after you've just had your abdomen sliced open and stitched back up. I implored everyone to cool it with the snappy banter, but when you have a bunch of wiseacres for friends, an occasional guffaw is going to erupt. It's inevitable. Other than when I was a preadolescent in synagogue, this was the only time in my life I didn't want to laugh.

Laughter made the pain spike but, unless I was doped up on Demerol, the dagger in the gut dogged me constantly. I couldn't move, go to the bathroom, or eat anything other than applesauce and Jell-O—all of which depressed me. I knew it was irrational to fear that I'd never recover, that I'd be stuck in this hospital bed forever, yet that's exactly the anxious shadow that loomed over me. The nurses carefully controlled my intake of Demerol, a necessary precaution for a highly addictive opiate. At the time, though, their parsimony pissed me off.

The following day dawned a bit better. The default level of pain ebbed a few clicks and my gastrointestinal system had improved to the point where I could start experimenting with solid food. A few people were lurking around at dinnertime, including my ever-present mother (love you, Mom!) and my witty CGQ drummer friend, Jim G.

The food dude brought me a tray rife with mystery. My guests ogled as I ceremoniously removed the metallic lid. There on the innocent plate lounged a rectangular chunk of grayish stuff (fish?), submerged in a swamp of indeterminate fluid, flanked by a clump of limp green beans and half a baked potato. It looked aggressively disgusting.

"Ah, I see you ordered the square fish," quipped my deadpan pal Jim.

Now, I don't know why, but that bit busted me up. I couldn't stop guffawing. And weeping. In that moment, I truly understood the phrase "to die laughing." Jim felt guilty for causing me this distress, but in his defense, I hadn't warned him about the dangers of post-abdominal surgery humor. On the other hand, even if I had, he probably couldn't have resisted the opportunity. That's one of the things I loved about him.

And, yeah, I know. The line wasn't *that* funny. Maybe my reaction was an unanticipated opportunity to release some of the stress of that daunting week. I'd been able to keep my shit together during the daytimes, when there was a lot of activity. But the nights were rough. Alone, I ruminated on what life was going to look like when I recovered enough physically to go home. Those thoughts weren't filled with lollipops and roses. Or square fish.

Before this academic year, which was supposed to be my last, I'd agreed to work as the music librarian for the DePaul Symphony in exchange for a partial tuition credit. The job entailed setting up and tearing down all the chairs and music stands for rehearsals as well as toting massive boxes of music to and from the rehearsal hall. No way was I going to be able to do any of that anytime soon. I'd been told to expect to be out of commission for at least a month. Would the school revoke my credit if I couldn't work for that long? Maybe they'd kick me out altogether if I missed too many classes or rehearsals. I'd already failed at college once and would be mortified to flake out again.

And what about my gigs? I was playing two nights a week at the Pump Room with Peter. I had that steady Monday-night jazz gig with Joe Daley. I worked most Saturday nights with one wedding band or another. All of that could easily disappear if I couldn't play. I'd fought hard for my financial independence, and at the age of twenty-five, I'd be damned if I was going to beg my divorced parents for rent money.

Wednesday morning a sadistic ogre (aka Nurse Blue) insisted I get up and walk to the bathroom and back, a grand total of twenty feet. When I sat up, I was certain my entrails were going to splat all over the floor. The nurse helped me to my feet and I shuffled to the bathroom, one hand clutching the IV pole, the other holding my remaining organs in.

How was I supposed to go home in two days when I was still in so much pain and so immobile? How would I survive when everyone else returned to their normal lives?

These unanswerable questions were no laughing matter.

Dinner and a Show

April 1981

"**D**o you want to play eight weeks of *Bye Bye Birdie*?"

It had only been a few days since I'd inched my way upstairs to my apartment after my stay at Saint Francis Hospital when I received this call. I was in no condition to play anything.

"When would this be?" I asked, trying to calm the tremolo in my voice.

"Let's see, opening night would be September first," Donald Miller, music director for Candlelight Dinner Playhouse, said. "You'll be taking over for John Floeter; he's a friend of yours, right?"

"Um—"

"And, if you do a great job, there will be other shows I'd need you for."

I did some quick mental calculating. September, hmm, that's five months from now. Surely I'll be fine by then, right? I tried to squelch the chorus of what-ifs screeching in my mind's ear. I hadn't ever considered making theater work my professional focus, but five-plus years of scuffling since dropping out of Northwestern had left a bitter residue in my heart and checking account. A reliable paycheck for two months and maybe more? When was an opportunity like this ever going to come around again?

"Sure, Don, I'd be glad to do it."

"Oh, excellent. John spoke very highly of you. I'm thrilled you're available."

"Me too," I said, hoping I wasn't lying my ass off.

John was the guy I'd met in the hallway outside Mr. Benfield's office the day of my first lesson. I guess he thought I could handle this gig. Cool. Maybe he'd even talked it over with Mr. B., who'd agreed I was a good fit for the Candlelight job.

Perhaps things were turning around for me. I knew I was "right place, right time" lucky to get called for this job, and having said yes, I was determined to prove to everyone, including myself, that I could ace *Bye Bye Birdie* and score future work at Candlelight. What's that warmth rising inside me? Oh yeah, I believe it's called hope.

Jazz Camp: I Am Not Bob Bowman

June 1981

Exactly two months after the appendicitis attack, I arrived on the campus of Emporia State University, bass and suitcase in tow. I was still treading tentatively and lifting things with caution. The midsummer Kansas heat scorched my lungs and fried my brain. I figured I'd better stay inside with the arctic air conditioning as much as possible during my week-long sojourn amidst the cornfields, hog farms, and jar stores.

The camp director had called me to play and teach at the Clark Terry Great Plains Jazz Camp on the recommendation of my drummer friend and benefactor Jack Mouse. What I didn't know was that I'd been hired to replace Bob Bowman, who, like Jack, was a native Kansan, and who'd accepted then bowed out of the camp gig. First, the van driver sent to pick me up at the airport, then literally everyone else, called me Bob for the first few days in Emporia. His name was in the camp's brochures as well as in the printed programs for the week's nightly big band concerts.

"Hey, Bob!"

"Good to meet you, Bob."

"Wait, you're not Bob?"

This mistaken identity nonsense made me chuckle at first (ha, ha, how silly!) but after a while I grew dark and defensive.

Damn it, stop it already. I'll succeed or fail myself, with my own name, thank you.

My thoughts were clouded with self-doubt long before I had to contend with this "I'm not Bob" bullshit. This jazz camp thing was *terra incognita* to me. I'd heard about National Stage Band Camps and the camps run by a guy called Jamey Aebersold, but I'd never attended one as a student. This would be my first as a faculty member.

I'd barely recovered from major surgery. Clark Terry was the first big-name jazz guy I was going to have the opportunity to play with. Was I going to make it or screw things up?

The camp's namesake was one of the true giants of the genre, having mastered swing and bebop styles on both trumpet and flugelhorn. Clark had played with Count Basie, Duke Ellington, Quincy Jones, Oscar Peterson, Dizzy Gillespie, and so many other heavy cats. He'd been a member of *The Tonight Show* band for ten years, so he was no stranger to celebrity. I was Mr. Nobody.

The very first night of that very first camp, I unexpectedly found myself playing a trumpet/bass duet on a Bb blues with Clark in the middle of a faculty big band concert. I got so nervous that I made the rookie mistake of trying to interact with C.T. using what jazz musicians call a "broken time feel." This is a style of playing where the rhythm section (in this case, just me) engages in a musical conversation with the soloist, instead of chugging along with a standard four-beats-to-the-bar pulse. This kind of interplay was pioneered around 1960 by Bill Evans's most famous trio, which featured the paradigm-busting bassist Scott LaFaro and the empathic drummer Paul Motian. I'd been learning how to play this way with Peter.

C.T. did not dig my broken time feel *at all*. He wanted me to walk straight 4/4 quarter notes while he did his thing, which he indicated by pointedly removing the horn from his lips and jabbing the air above his head with all four fingers of his right hand. I mentally slapped myself upside the head.

Of course! Clark was old school. I should have known not to jump in with this more modern approach for our impromptu duet—especially on that first night. Maybe I'd have considered this more carefully if I'd had advance warning, but jazz is all about improvisation. You have to make spontaneous decisions about what to play every moment, tempered by knowledge, taste, experience, and instinct. Part of that calculus has to include knowing who you're playing with and what role that person will likely want you to play. I booted my chance to make a positive first impression on Clark and the rest of the band. *Shit.*

Most of my time in Emporia was going to be spent teaching middle and high school kids from the Corn Belt. Though I'd taken on a few individual students here and there previously, I had zero experience teaching group bass lessons, nor had I ever coached jazz combos, tasks that were at the core of my camp responsibilities.

Everyone has to start somewhere, but even with my private students in Chicago I often felt like the awkward first-year grade school instructor who survives by staying one chapter in the textbook ahead of his students.

A typical bass class had me perched awkwardly on the edge of a desk in front of a blackboard, facing a dozen pimply-faced kids (mostly boys), each of whom thought they knew way more than I did. Apparently, they thought I was Mr. Nobody, too.

"OK," I'd yell. "Let's get tuned up, alright?"

There'd be an explosion of rumbling and snapping and popping as a few of the students gamely tried to tune while the others flailed away on their bass guitars. Precious minutes would pass as I attempted to restore some semblance of order.

"Who knows how to walk a twelve-bar blues?" I'd finally ask, searching for an opening gambit that might spark their interest.

I tried to pass along what I'd gleaned from the few short years I'd put in as a fledgling jazz and commercial freelancer. Mostly, I made shit up as I stumbled along. There was some wiggle room for my naïveté with these less-experienced students. I knew there were gaping holes in my bass technique and understanding of harmony, but I had to pretend otherwise to survive the heat I felt from the kids, Clark, and the faculty.

After that first ignominious performance with Clark, I hid in the weeds like a good little boy as much as possible for the remainder of the camp's concerts. I don't know how Bob Bowman would have fared in this situation, but at least I stopped sweating comparisons to him by camp's end.

The fourteen-hour days, my still tender belly, and the ever-present feelings of inferiority conspired to make this one week of jazz camp hella interminable. Yet I must have done well enough to impress the camp director. After the final night's concert, he invited me to return the next summer, an offer I accepted straightaway.

When I showed up the following June, I wore a tee shirt bearing the inscription "I Am Not Bob Bowman."

Onstage at the Clark Terry Great Plains Jazz Camp

Dems Da Breaks

1981–1982

It's my first time on a baseball diamond since Little League. I'm standing near first base among a group of mostly twenty-something musicians on Sunday afternoon, June 28, 1981. We're tossing a sixteen-inch softball around and ribbing each other about how out of shape we all are. No one's wearing a mitt; that's the rule for sixteen-inch. It's a game for tough guys. Or those who like to think they are.

Someone grabs a bat and starts swatting grounders to the infielders, who scoop them up and chuck the ball to me at first. I catch the first few pegs without mishap, then the batter taps one to third base, where Rick Frigo, the drummer in Peter's trio, is patrolling. He charges the ball à la Ron Santo and flings it at me, hard. I reach for the ball, fingers splayed. It slams into the tip of my left-hand index finger with a sickening crack and caroms off into the dirt.

I crumple to my knees. Right away I know it's bad. Very bad. *Goddammit. Why didn't I keep my fingers together?* Before any of my friends can react, I pick myself up and stride, head down, toward my car, parked on the perimeter of the field.

"Hey, man, you all right?"

"Did you hurt yourself?"

"Where you going?"

"What happened?" asks Peter, who has run to catch up with me.

I shake my head. I can't look at him. I can't look at any of them. I flop into the driver's seat, and jerk the door shut. *I've got to get the hell away from here as fast as this piece of shit car can go.* I rip out of the parking space and speed home without a word to anyone.

As soon as I walk in the door to my apartment, I bury my hand in a bucket of ice. After half an hour, the finger is purple and bulbous and sending shock waves to my brain. Something more has to be done, but I can't think what. I call my girlfriend Lindy, who must be getting tired of playing nursemaid for me. She comes over, takes one look at my mangled digit, blanches, and whisks me to the nearest emergency room. Here we go again.

Soon I'm seesawing on an exam table at Grant Hospital, waiting for the Novocain to kick in. Dr. Sidell, the orthopedic surgeon on duty, enters and slides a sheet of X-ray prints onto a backlit screen. He emits a low whistle.

"What do you do for a living, Mr. Harrison?"

"I'm an upright bass player."

The doctor, inexplicably, chuckles. When he sees the *what the fuck is so funny* expression on my face, he stifles the laughter.

"Oh. Sorry. You're not kidding? Well, uh, this is serious. The X-rays show that you've got an interstitial fracture. A small chunk of bone has broken off and is floating inside the joint of the middle knuckle. See this little white blotch? There's a fifty-fifty chance you'll need to have surgery to remove that bit. We won't know for a week or so."

A nauseating dread rises in my throat. I catch Lindy's eye; she furrows an eyebrow then looks away. Without warning, the doctor performs a jiu-jitsu twist on my finger.

"Ow! Damn."

"Sorry about that. A heads-up before that treatment doesn't usually do any good."

Sidell tapes a metal splint to my finger and anchors it with a cast that engulfs my entire hand and wrist.

"Your finger's going to be immobilized for at least four weeks."

"Jesus ..."

"This is a bad break, Mr. Harrison. What happened?"

"I was playing sixteen-inch softball. Actually, we weren't even playing yet."

"Maybe not the best thing to do if you're a musician?"

"Yeah, I know." *Gimme a break, man. It was an accident.* "Can you cut away some of this cast? I need to use the other fingers in the meantime."

I figure three fingers are better than none, and since bass guitar is a bit easier on the hands than upright, I might be able to get away with playing electric bass on some of my upcoming gigs. I can't afford another extended period with no income.

How the hell did I agree to play ball without a mitt? I told myself it was a stupid idea but did it anyway. The other guys, most of them professional musicians, didn't behave as if playing sixteen-inch was much of a risk, so why should I? I didn't want to be seen as a wuss. Proving I wasn't afraid was evidently more important than safeguarding my hands.

Which is how I found myself in the utterly avoidable predicament of being a twenty-five-year-old kid facing a potentially career-ending injury.

I didn't talk about this with anyone. Not Lindy, not my mother, not Peter, not any of my other friends. Instead, I shoved all the anger, shame, fear, and self-recrimination into that bucket of ice along with my hand. The knee-jerk macho tapes reverberated in my head:

Nobody gives a shit about your little broken finger. Suck it up, man. Go about your business and don't go looking for sympathy. No one respects a man who's weak or needy.

As Dr. Sidell had predicted, the index finger was unusable for nearly four weeks. I downed handfuls of ibuprofen in a marginally successful attempt to manage the pain, which ebbed and flowed in unpredictable waves. X-rays taken one week after the incident showed I wouldn't need surgery—a lucky break. A week after that, the most intense misery had subsided enough for me to make a few gigs on electric bass. In my anxious brain, I was hurting more for money than from the broken finger at that point. I got some concerned looks from other musicians when I showed up with a cast on my hand and only three fingers available for duty. They were mercifully understanding as I bumbled my way through those jobs.

On July 24, I returned to Grant Hospital to meet with Dr. Sidell's colleague, Dr. Newman. He sawed off the cast and delicately removed the splint. The chilly air prickled the parts of my hand that had been under wraps for all that time. The skin was the bluish white of powdered skim milk. I tried to move the index finger but all it did was twitch. I looked at Dr. Newman with alarm.

"You have, um, *had* hyper-toned muscles in your finger," the doctor explained. "They atrophied—lost their strength much faster than normal muscles when you abruptly stopped using them."

"What does that mean?"

"Well, it means you're going to have to work extra hard to regain some range of motion and muscle tone."

"How do I do that? I've got a steady theater gig a couple of months from now."

Something flickered on the surgeon's face.

"I'm sorry to have to tell you this, but I can't guarantee you'll ever have the same mobility and strength as before."

I stared dumbly into space for a long moment.

"Look, here's what you do. Get yourself some Silly Putty—the stuff you played with as a kid? Roll it between your finger and thumb; squeeze it, flatten it out. Play with it any old way, just be sure to involve the index finger as best you can."

"I can't even move it, so—"

"You have to be patient. It's going to hurt. There's still considerable inflammation in the joint, which will diminish over time. You can also practice making a fist when you get tired of the Silly Putty."

"Yeah. That's what I feel like doing most of the time anyway."

"I don't doubt it. Come back in a couple of weeks and we'll evaluate your progress."

I spent the next few days squishing Silly Putty and flexing my hand open and shut hundreds of times. It was obvious that I'd lost a lot of strength since I'd last played the upright bass. I understood the doctor's advice about being patient but I needed to find out what I was up against.

So, one morning, I picked up my bass, balanced it against my left thigh and abdomen, and placed all four fingers on a string. I pressed down.

Fuck, that's hard.

Next came the acid test: I tried to depress the string with only my first finger. A searing stab of agony shot from the injured knuckle the instant I applied the slightest pressure. I laid the bass on its side, then laid myself on the couch with my right arm slung over my wet face.

There was no time to wallow. My job at Candlelight was right around the corner. If I played well, Don might want me to work at the theater for many months to come. This could be my lucky break. I wanted to be a full-time professional musician, and this was my opportunity, broken finger be damned.

The theater schedule would be grueling: eight shows in five days each week, with doubles on Wednesdays, Saturdays, and Sundays. Somehow, I had to rebuild my strength and stamina essentially from zero. And it had to happen fast. Was this moment going to be the end of a career that had barely begun, or the launch of one that was revving up? The answer was in my hands, literally.

Meanwhile, my calendar for July and August was loaded with rehearsals, gigs, and schoolwork. I resumed working two nights a week with Peter's trio at the Pump Room. I'd hired a sub to cover the initial two weeks after the softball debacle, then returned as a three-fingered bass guitarist. There were plenty of technical things I couldn't do without my strongest finger but Peter and Rick, the guy who'd flung that softball to me, graciously cut me a lot of slack.

During the day I was busy playing catch-up with the latter half of spring semester at DePaul—attending classes, taking bass and piano lessons, cranking out papers, and completing exams for three graduate-level classes. When was I going to find time to practice?

In addition, I was supposed to fly to Winnipeg on August 15 to perform and teach at the Saskatchewan Summer School for the Arts for a week. I was still limited to playing electric bass, much to the not-so-silent disdain of some of my fellow faculty. Shortly after returning I was scheduled to close on a condo I was purchasing, with a loan for the down payment from my mother. Moving day was going to be August 31. My first show at Candlelight would be the very next day.

If this all sounds insane, it was.

I bulled my way through the persistent aching and swelling in my knuckle. As my debut performance of *Bye Bye Birdie* approached, it was clear I wasn't going to be ready. I'd have to confront the situation in teeth-gritting mode.

The first dozen shows were horrendous. I panicked at the top of every Act I:

Is this the show I won't get through?

I did my best to hide both the pain and the anxiety from the music director and the other musicians. Once again, I didn't want anyone to get the impression I was weak or incompetent. Months later, after he'd hired me for the next show, Don, the music director, told me he'd thought my playing was "anemic" at first. I'd neglected to mention that I was rehabbing from an injury until I was sure I'd secured the job.

By week three, things were turning around. I stopped having to secretly soak my hand in ice water after each show and I was able to cut down on the ibuprofen. When I saw Dr. Sidell for our final appointment in late September, he was surprised how much I'd improved.

"Not many people are able to regain this much use after an injury like yours. You must have put in a lot of effort."

Yes, I had. The Candlelight gig had forced me to spend many more hours playing the bass than I would have otherwise. Pain or no pain, I'd said yes. I needed the money, and I thought this show could be the springboard for the career I wanted. When those initial eight weeks stretched into the better part of a year, I grew accustomed to the diminished level of anxiety made possible by a regular income.

I doubt I would have recovered the serviceable use of my index finger had it not been for these circumstances, which would have put an end to my dream of being a professional musician. Somehow, I'd made the best of the bad break in order to take advantage of the good one.

Part III

Sideman

1982–1995

My datebooks from the 1980s are filled with what my father used to call "chicken scratches," a remnant of my failure to develop legible penmanship as a kid. The dense black-and-blue scrawl covers nearly every square inch of those calendars. Flipping through them reminds me how those years set the tone for what was to come for the next quarter century.

I worked my frickin' butt off. After six more months at Candlelight Theater—thirteen weeks each of *Oklahoma!* and *Zorba*—I cobbled together a freelance income doing a hodgepodge of work in four main categories I came to think of as pillars for survival: jobbing, jazz, teaching, and musical theater. I participated in "the gig economy" years before that phrase became part of the zeitgeist.

The largest chunk of my income, whether I liked it or not, came from jobbing. Though I wasn't an entirely enthusiastic participant in the process, working in multiple jobbing bands under a panoply of circumstances transformed me into a competent sideman.

A sideman (a term for which there isn't a gender-neutral equivalent) is a musician who accompanies (or *plays beside*) a leader or headliner. Qualifications for jobbing sidemen include technical proficiency on your instrument(s) (including the ability to play a variety of musical styles), knowledge of the standard repertoire, and awareness of your place in the musical hierarchy.

My first step in the direction of marketability as a commercial bassist was getting my electric bass chops together, since 90 percent of jobbing calls for electric, not upright, bass. I'd played electric exclusively for *Zorba* during my final three months at Candlelight, so my increased level of comfort with the instrument was mostly the result of on-the-job experience. Once again, due to my persistent pigheadedness, I wouldn't have put in the effort to improve on the bass guitar had there not been compelling reasons to do so.

In-demand sidemen have to be hip to the standard repertoire, an ever-evolving list of songs you're going to have to play no matter who you work for. When I entered the business, the canon of jobbing fare stretched well back into the 1940s. It included music from the big band era; Broadway show tunes; pop and rock from the '50s, '60s and '70s; Motown; plus a full complement of disco hits. Here's a random sample: "String of Pearls," "Hello Dolly," "You Are the Sunshine of My Life," "Proud Mary," "I Will Survive," "Jumpin' Jack Flash," "Stayin' Alive," "Just the Way You Are," "Billie Jean," and both songs with the title "Time after Time." And let us not forget the ubiquitous "Celebration," a song that overstayed its welcome like your soused Uncle Ned at Thanksgiving.

The final essential quality for competence as a sideman is understanding and accepting your role in the jobbing juggernaut. You're never the star of the show; you're a member of the supporting cast, like B. J. Armstrong or Horace Grant to Michael Jordan. You may be asked to step out into the spotlight for a few seconds to sink a key three-pointer, but the bulk of your job is done in relative obscurity. This is a bitter pill for some musicians to swallow but I savored the obscurity of jobbing with gratitude. For me these dates were like commando raids: get in, make the low notes, and get out.

Sometimes getting in and out of the venue was the hardest part of the job. I played private parties in hotel ballrooms (ranging from cheesy to ritzy), bars, restaurants, suburban wedding-factory banquet halls, and every imaginable kind of setting in between. Navigating the path to each bandstand presented its own challenges, some more labyrinthine than others.

Two of the toniest downtown joints, the Ritz-Carlton Hotel and the Drake Hotel, were notorious among musicians for having horrifying load-ins. The Drake was the most menacing of the two. After dragging your gear up a steeply inclined sidewalk to their loading dock, jockeying for position with other musicians and miscellaneous vendors, you had to brave the Hill of Death. This was a thirty-yard, twenty-degree downhill ramp leading to the hotel's elevators. There are drummers who've been running to catch up with their trap cases since 1998 in that hellhole.

Often, traveling to the venue's banquet room entailed hauling your equipment through a treacherous kitchen. Floors were slippery with grease, passageways were narrow, and you'd find yourself weaving between cooks, waiters, busboys, and harried room managers, all of whom had urgent business directly in your path.

The Ritz-Carlton's chaotic kitchen was a particularly egregious example. It was especially aggravating because the route to the kitchen was so lengthy and circuitous to begin with. After entering the building through double security doors (quite the neat trick with a double bass in tow), you'd take an elevator down two levels. You'd show your ID and sign in at their security desk, then walk two city blocks to another bank of elevators. You'd ride up to the twelfth floor, typically with a surly hotel employee who resents your very existence, then traverse the same two blocks through the kitchen (which looks like rush hour in the Tokyo subway) to get to the Grand Ballroom or whatever the hell they call it. With a tip of the chapeau to the film "Office Space," that place sucks.

The setting for one memorable wedding I played was a south suburban Rotary-type club. Rob, the guitarist/singer/leader, Jules, the drummer, and I knew something was up as soon as we wheeled our equipment into the club's party room. The joint would have been the ideal setting for a small-town slasher movie. Everything was drab. The odor of mold and Old Style hung in the air.

We set up on a badly-in-need-of-refinishing auditorium stage. I worried that our amps would blow out their fuse box. As we readied ourselves, someone carried in a long Formica table, the kind you might see at a church potluck, and positioned it on the floor in front of the stage. Then they laid out dozens of plastic shot glasses, along with several bottles of Jim Beam. The three of us gave one another the universal side-eye expression for *What the fuck is this?*

People filtered in, dressed liked they were attending a barbecue—not shorts and tee shirts, but almost. The band, overdressed in our sport coats and ties, eased into our first set of innocuous bossa novas and polite pop tunes. Not fifteen minutes later, someone called out

"Beam me!" and guests rushed to the table and threw back a shot. I'd never seen anything remotely like this.

Uh-oh. If they keep this up, we'll be lucky to get out of here alive.

And keep it up they did. Throughout the remainder of the evening, random people would shout "Beam me!" at random moments. Luckily, once Rob broke out the Rolling Stones and Steppenwolf repertoire, the increasingly inebriated guests staggered onto what passed for a dance floor and gyrated to our music.

At least they like us. For now.

At some point, a guest slur-yelled, "Freebird!" and the cry was taken up by several other wobbly party-goers.

"Well, that didn't take long," Rob told us, his back facing the unrulier-by-the-minute crowd. Taking no chances, he launched right into "Jumpin' Jack Flash," which mollified the crowd.

When we finished our final set, we heard the inevitable calls to "Play one more!" Then came the chanting, "One more song! One more song!" Rob led us in an abbreviated version of "Gimme Some Lovin'," after which we put down our instruments and started packing up. The crowd got the message that we were done for good.

We absquatulated out of there as fast as humanly possible. The three of us reconnoitered in the parking lot. Rob had procured the check and we were safely out of the danger zone.

"Well, this is one for the annals," I said. "I can see the headline now: 'Wedding Band Survives Satanic Beam Me Ritual in South Suburbs.'"

"Yeah, tonight was more like a circus than a jobbing gig," Rob said, then added his oft-repeated post-gig call to arms: "Come the revolution, there'll be no more jobbing dates, fish-faced enemy of the people!"

Jules, the most stoic member of the trio, shook his head and wordlessly ambled to his car.

On the drive home, snippets of the evening intermingled with bits of memories of that first gig I played in the bowling alley with Korky and Ted.

Humility, my friend. That's your takeaway from this one.

Anyone can play a cushy job in a fancy ballroom; it takes a real jobbing warrior to make it through gigs like this.

As the venues ran the gamut, so did the cast of characters I worked for in the 1980s. I was fortunate to get hired by predominantly decent people, who would communicate honestly and directly. There were a few doozies out there as well, leaders who would lie and cheat both their clients and sidemen in creative and nefarious ways. It took a while for me to learn which bandleaders I couldn't trust.

Some of these guys (yes, they were mostly dudes) would "forget" to pay for overtime or take an inordinately long time to mail a check. One leader didn't pay me for more than a year, despite my numerous attempts to reach out to him. Aggravated beyond reason, I sent this nitwit a self-addressed stamped envelope, which he ignored. Another bandleader, an otherwise nice guy, was infamous for taking forever to pay his sidemen. Once I sussed this out, I insisted he pay me in cash or money order at the start of every gig. I don't know why, but he faithfully acquiesced to this demand.

One of the worst repeat offenders was a bandleader I'll call T, who I still fear might stir up trouble if I expose their name or gender. This person would give me a batch of dates as "holds" (when there were gigs allegedly pending), most of which would later fall through. When I'd call to check on the status of a "hold," T would retort, "I never had a gig on that date." They would also regularly send paychecks that were ten or twenty dollars less than the fee we'd originally agreed upon. When pressed, T would say something like "I never agreed to that rate. The gig pays [whatever the amount of the check was]." I eventually got it through my thick skull that this person was a pathological liar.

Any sideman who was in the commercial music business during this era in Chicago will surely recognize the names of my frequent employers: Steve Miles, who'd put on his tuxedo first thing in the morning on the day of a gig because he didn't like to change clothes; Al Stevens, whose partner Mario would hold an upright bass on the bandstand but didn't actually play it; Ray Sassetti, whose name I first misheard as Racist Eddy; and Georgia Frances, a complicated soul. My friend Peter booked his share of jobbing dates as well. I played as many of them as I could, as it was always better to be among friends.

The most appallingly problematic bandleader of all made a practice of sending out multiple bands on a given night without necessarily telling his clients that he wouldn't be at the job personally to run the show. He'd skim a felonious percentage off the top then pay someone to sub-lead the group for him. After a couple of years of working for him as a sideman, that someone became me.

I stupidly allowed myself to be put in the awkward position of having to, essentially, pretend to be this guy on several occasions when I sub-led a band for him. I dreaded those gigs. I was supposed to take charge of the situation with confidence, like the Muppet Guy Smiley. Instead, I dragged my bones to and from the venues like a zombie. When I arrived home after these jobs I felt as if I needed to take several showers to cleanse the ethical filth.

At one lavish North Shore wedding, the father of the bride, an almost-ringer for Eugene Levy, barged up to the bandstand while we were assembling our gear.

"Where's _____?" he demanded.

"Uh, he's not here this evening."

"Well, fer crissake. I paid for his orchestra to play my daughter's wedding. Who the hell are you? Are you guys even any good?"

I couldn't blame him for being steamed. I fudged the best answer I could come up with on the fly.

"We work with _____ all the time. If you give us a chance, I think you'll be happy with our performance."

"This better be good or I'm not paying a dime."

It so happened that I'd booked a crack band that particular night, with an excellent (and dangerously good-looking) female singer. We kept the dance floor full all evening, which was the yardstick I used to gauge success at these events. Afterwards, Big Daddy, who I spied ogling the vocalist a time or two, gave me a check without complaint.

However, this was the end of the line for me with this *gonif* band-leader. If I'd absorbed only one lesson from my jobbing journey thus far, it was that I had to act less from a position of desperation (I'll do *anything* for a gig), and more from a standpoint that took into account my improving skill set and decreasing tolerance for bullshit from employers. Being a successful sideman didn't have to mean giving up my autonomy. Or integrity.

The Bickersons

1983–1986

O nce I figured out where I stood with them, I had WYSIWYG (what you see is what you get) business relationships with most of the bandleaders I worked for throughout the '80s and '90s.

Not so with Georgia Frances and her husband, John Bishop. John was a talented jazz guitarist who had been making a living playing clubs in Chicago and on the road. Georgia probably could have had a fine career as a classical violinist. Instead, they found one another and began operating the Georgia Frances Orchestra, a jobbing band with a highfalutin name, in the early 1980s. My relationship with them was anything but WYSIWYG.

After a brief introductory phone call, Georgia invited me to drop by their five-night steady gig to hear the group and say hello. One evening in early 1983, I went to check them out in the atrium lobby of the Hyatt Regency Hotel. Three violinists, a pianist, and a guitarist were sailing through "The Blue Danube Waltz," a piece I'd come to know as a Georgia Frances Orchestra staple. It was immediately clear which of the fiddle players was Georgia. She was around five six. I could tell she'd once been beautiful. Now she appeared unwell, with an ashen complexion and a body that exuded the heaviness of exhaustion. As if to belie her mien, Georgia's playing crackled with energy and power. She stood between the other two violinists, who faded into the background in Georgia's presence.

John, standing behind the string players, had a similarly ghoulish skin tone, as if neither he nor his wife ever went outdoors. His playing, though, was as strong as he appeared physically weak. John's face was puffy, like the Pillsbury Doughboy's, and he carried with him an aura of defeat.

Georgia and John were blessed with an abundance of musical talent and cursed with an equal measure of anxiety. They drank coffee and smoked cigarettes incessantly. My flutist friend Marc, who occasionally worked for them, once quipped, "I'd like to have a conversation with John, if only he'd stop vibrating."

After the waltz, the quintet played "Eine Kleine Nachtmusik." This was certainly not your typical schlocky hotel bar band. After the set, I approached them to introduce myself.

"Georgia? Hi, I'm Bill."

"Oh, hi. I wasn't sure you'd come down. This is Marsha and Naomi. That's Greg at the piano."

The guitarist stepped forward. "Hey, Bill. John Bishop." We shook hands all around. "Come hang out with us on our so-called break."

I trailed after them through a maze of escalators and hallways. Georgia sat me down with her, Greg, and the other violinists. John made a beeline for a remote corner of the break room. I noted that the couple neither sat together nor exchanged any words during this intermission, which seemed odd.

The following week, I played my first Hyatt gig with the GFO.

"How 'bout we play 'Just the Two of Us'?" John asked mildly, midway through our first set.

Georgia spun around with fire in her eyes and hissed, "No, absolutely not. We're going to do 'Edelweiss.'"

John stared wearily ahead. "Alright."

Wait, what? I couldn't believe the little scene I'd just observed. Were they kidding? Judging from the "not this again" look on Greg's face, the couple was dead serious. Later the pianist whispered that "it was only a matter of time" before Georgia and John would go through what he called their "routine."

"This isn't the worst of it," Greg warned. "Wait and see."

The band was on a strictly regimented schedule—forty minutes on, twenty minutes off. Hotel management wanted us to disappear during breaks, so we had to cool our heels in that far-away break room. After three sets, I felt like a yo-yo. There was neither a bandstand nor an audience per se in the lobby. We were tucked away near the escalator, not on any sort of stage. Guests might catch snippets of a song while they were going up, down, in, or out. Other than the draconian time boundaries, the gig seemed like it should have had a fairly relaxed vibe.

Yet John and Georgia treated the job as if it were a high-wire act. Everything was geared toward the band looking just so. The women wore incongruously fancy ball gowns; the men, tuxedoes. One tightly held rule was that there be little or no pauses between pieces. When any small thing went awry, the coleaders were ill equipped to take it in stride. They were like a pair of scrappy, screeching alley cats who constantly had their hackles up, as if they were scuffling over one scrawny mouse. Georgia was usually the aggressor; John either remained silent or pushed back with quiet vehemence.

A typical conflict on a dance gig with their full jobbing band went something like this:

"Pull up number seventeen," John would tell the band, sending us diving through their gigantic library to find that particular arrangement.

"No! We're doing number eighty-three," Georgia would practically spit. Back we'd go to dig for chart eighty-three.

"OK," John would acquiesce, rolling his eyes. "Ready with eighty-three? Ah-one, ah-two—"

"One, two, one, two, three, four," Georgia would yell, at a faster tempo than John had started counting. This would lead to considerable confusion among us hapless sidemen. Who should we follow?

Peter worked with the couple on and off during my tenure. He's the one who came up with the wholly appropriate nickname for Georgia and John: the Bickersons.

When John and Georgia's sparring kicked into gear I wouldn't know where to look. I'd steal a glance at Mark, the drummer, or Greg, the keyboard player, then maybe pretend to adjust my amp or fiddle with my bow tie. What I really wanted to do was sneak offstage unseen and hide in the men's room until hostilities ceased. I could only hope that this time would be a skirmish and not a pitched battle.

Their volatility was troubling but there were certain qualities about these two people that drew me to them. As much as their conflict repulsed me, it also elicited compassion. Their anxiety was palpable. They exacerbated each other's stress and jangled the nerves of everyone around them. Perhaps I was attracted to them because I thought I could help them in some way.

In rare relaxed moments John could be surprisingly gentle and charming. He might wax poetic about his favorite guitarist, Wes Montgomery, or tell me how much he enjoyed my playing. And, once in a great while, Georgia would expose the vulnerable underbelly of her personality she normally kept under wraps. One night, when I happened to be the first sideman to arrive at the gig, she sidled up to me and said, in the sweetest tone of voice,

"You may be rock and roll on the outside but you're Beethoven on the inside."

I have no idea what that meant but it sure made me feel warm and fuzzy—until she and John were at each other's throats an hour later.

One engagement for Georgia and John tested my limits in a different way. On occasion, a bandleader might ask sidemen to don a Hawaiian shirt, a plaid vest, or a goofy hat for a particular gig. On December 13, 1983, Peter and I were two of at least a dozen musicians the Bickersons hired for a corporate extravaganza at the Hyatt that played out like a scene from a Buñuel film. The party planners had us report to the venue ninety minutes before the downbeat. Their minions costumed us like the Coneheads, those lovable

December 13, 1983

alien characters (played by Dan Aykroyd and Jane Curtin) from Saturday Night Live, circa 1977–79. With tuxedos.

The absurdity of that gig was an apt analogy for how ridiculous working with John and Georgia became. It was impossible to know what sort of people they'd been before they turned their marriage into a business, but this version of the Bickersons was dysfunctional in ways that embarrassed me for them and for myself when I shared a stage with them.

I cut ties with Georgia and John in 1986. Enough was enough. My patience and empathy had worn too thin to salvage. I had to relegate them to my personal "do not play with or for" list.

The last time I saw the Bickersons was around '89, while working at the Chicago Hilton and Towers with Peter and Rick. Between sets, I wandered toward the main entrance of the hotel on Michigan Avenue. There, under the glare of the hotel's marquee, I spied John and Georgia through the large plate glass window, waiting for their car to be delivered by the valet. Although I couldn't hear her voice, I could see that Georgia was rebuking her husband nonstop while he stood by impassively, waiting for the storm to blow over. They were still frozen in that sad tableau when I headed back to the bandstand.

I Sling the Body Electric

1971–2017

'd been eyeballing Tony's bass guitar for a month or two, wondering how it might feel compared to Igor. Tony was the tall, enigmatic bassist and leader of a band called Sunnnngh. (Their silly name derived from the brand name Sunn, whose amplifiers the band used.) The group practiced in guitarist Bob's basement, where I'd sometimes hang out after school. My friend Phil and I roadied and mixed sound for them when they played shows.

One of these afternoons, I was at Bob's listening to Sunnnngh rehearse Cream's "Politician." The band took a break. This was the day I worked up the courage to approach Tony.

"Hey, man. Can I try your bass?"

"You? Yeah, OK. Just don't mess with my settings."

"Nah, I won't touch anything. How do I turn it on?"

"It's on, man. Just put the strap around your shoulder and have at it."

"Cool."

Tony's axe was heavier than it looked, which I discovered while hoisting it up to slip the strap over my head. The bass hung down around my knees, making it geometrically challenging to get ahold of the neck. I plucked an open E. *Boom!* The floor shook. I fretted a couple of notes. Ugh. They made an ugly buzzing noise. I thought playing acoustic bass was hard, but that thing was a beast in its own way. Tony handled the bass with such ease that I imagined it would be a breeze. It wasn't.

Some people, including many double bass players, think that switching from upright to electric is a no-brainer. That was my ill-informed view before I had a go at it. The bass guitar serves the same supportive rhythmic and harmonic function in a group as the upright bass, but it's a different animal altogether.

The bass guitar's neck is horizontal, not vertical, which makes the angles awkward for someone like me with short arms and stubby fingers. The scale is much shorter; a typical bass guitar has a thirty-four-inch neck versus the upright's approximately forty-inch *mensure*. That's not the physical advantage it sounds like because, ideally, you're supposed to play electric using one finger per fret. This was well-nigh impossible for me in the lowest positions, where the frets are a mile apart.

Both the position and the "touch" of the right hand are radically different from one instrument to the other. Upright jazz players place their first and second fingers of the right hand parallel to the strings and pull the string in the vertical plane (rather like a slingshot). Electric players attack the string at a ninety-degree angle, using more of the fingertips than double bassists do. The bass guitar requires a lighter touch, less brute force, more finesse. Thumb slapping presents a whole other set of challenges, which are exclusive to the electric (with rare exceptions like Stanley Clarke, who slaps the crap out of his upright).

Finally, there's the dang frets, those slender metal bars protruding from the fingerboard. They're supposed to be helpful. They just got in my way.

After my brief experiment with Tony's bass, I was leery about agreeing to play with some high school guys who were assembling a Chicago Transit Authority (later shortened to Chicago) cover band. CTA was one of the earliest big-name "fusion" bands, created by a group of musicians who met at DePaul University in the late '60s. They were one of the first rock-oriented groups to make saxophone, trumpet, and trombone an integral part of their sound. The invitation from those kids was the first time anyone thought I was cool enough to join their band. As hesitant as I was about my capability with the bass guitar, how could I say no? I borrowed a classmate's electric bass and hung in there as best I could. First time playing with a rock band. Check.

I bought my first electric bass, a beat-up fretless Fender Precision, around 1977, when I realized I had to arm myself for the kinds of gigs where the upright wouldn't cut it.

Why did I get a fretless? Not because I was trying to be like Jaco Pastorius, the virtuoso bassist/composer who had burst onto the scene with the release of his first album in 1976. Jaco's playing was an aspirational model for a generation of bassists, but I was sensible enough to know I'd never have those kinds of chops. No, I bought a fretless bass because I remembered the embarrassing clanking noises I'd made on Tony's bass. Of all the factors differentiating electric from upright, frets gave me the most trouble. I reasoned that a fretless electric would be a shrewd compromise.

However, the fretless sound was *not* what commercial band-leaders wanted. Frets impart a particular quality—call it solidity—to the sound of the bass guitar. Without the metal bars, fingers on a fret-free fingerboard produce a rich "mwah" tone with a soupçon of "growl" that's hard to describe. (Check out Jaco's astounding version of "Donna Lee" on his eponymous debut album for a quintessential example of the sound of a fretless Jazz bass.) Frets also guarantee that notes will be in tune. Fingers can fudge intonation; frets don't. I soon realized that a fretless Fender wasn't the optimal choice if I was only going to own one bass guitar.

I can't recall what happened to that instrument. What I do know is that I bought a fretted electric bass from Greg Mitchell's widow in 1981. Recall that Greg was the bassist I'd replaced in Peter's trio. His bass guitar was a vintage Fender, with a Precision neck attached to a Jazz body. It produced a delicious mix of clarity and woof. And it played like a cool summer night. This was the instrument I relied on while recovering from both the appendectomy and the broken index finger, when I was unable to lift heavy things or play upright bass.

The Mitchell Fender slipped out of my hands in a most unfortunate way. One Saturday night after an especially hellacious wedding job, I wheeled my flatbed cart full of gear out to my car, accompanied by my drummer friend Sarah Allen. The last piece of equipment I carefully placed on top of the pile of equipment was the bass.

Once outside, Sarah and I put our respective stuff in our vehicles and continued chatting. I stowed everything in my station wagon except the Fender, which I leaned up against the car, inches from where I stood. I said so long to Sarah, waltzed around to the driver's side door, hopped in, and drove off. I didn't realize that I'd neglected to put the bass in the car until I got home and began unloading.

I sped back to the venue's parking lot, but the bass was, of course, long gone. I totally lost my shit, kicking the car and whacking my head with clenched fists.

"You fucking idiot! What the hell is *wrong* with you," I screamed into the night.

Over the next few days, I put up signs throughout the neighborhood offering a reward, and haunted all the nearby music stores and pawnshops. I never saw that bass again.

I'd lost speakers and amps after foolishly leaving them vulnerable to thieves at venues and once, out of sheer exhaustion, in my car. Those losses impacted my wallet, not my soul. Losing a beloved instrument is a whole other thing. A bass isn't a person, of course, but that Fender had become part of my musical identity. I missed feeling its heft against my chest and the sleek coolness of its neck in my left palm. Its absence was like an amputation.

Letting go of a favorite instrument willingly, as I'd done with Igor and the honey-colored Mittenwald, is difficult enough. But a forcible parting like this is akin to the sudden death of a loved one. That may sound melodramatic, but the grief I felt after leaving that bass in the parking lot was palpable.

I don't know how common this is, nor do I understand it, but death and the presence or absence of instruments connected with the arc of my musical life several times. In Greg Mitchell's case, I wound up with his job *and* his electric bass, which was a disturbing mashup of good fortune and creepiness. I bought my next bass guitar in '88 from Rob Amster, an excellent bassist with mental health issues whose untimely death rocked the music community just a few years later.

Rob's bass was a baby-blue Yamaha five-string. He'd played it on tour with the fearsome drummer Buddy Rich, so it had seen some road by the time I acquired it. Playing a five-string (with a low B) had become *de rigueur* for jobbing bass players because so many pop tunes of that era had bass lines that extended down into that range. Four strings were bad enough; that B string confused the hell out of me.

Whenever I heard masterful bass guitar players like Paul McCartney, James Jamerson, Carol Kaye, Leland Sklar, and (of course) Jaco, the instrument sounded magnificent. After many years of hacking away at it, my electric playing remained lackluster; serviceable but unexceptional. There were a few periods when some creative project or a musical theater gig motivated me to invest practice time on the electric but I never had the kind of passion for the instrument that I did for the upright. Try as I might, I could never gin up the necessary enthusiasm.

As the types of work I was doing became more varied and plentiful, so did the bass guitars that passed through my hands. I bought, played, and sold instruments made by Fender, Yamaha, and Ibanez. Just after the turn of the twenty-first century, the blue Yamaha was plucked from the back seat of my garaged car by unknown miscreants. I was sorry to see it go, but that theft made me angry, not sad. I should have known by then never to leave anything valuable in a vehicle. As my grandmother Dorothy used to say, "Too soon oldt and too late schmart."

In 2002 I purchased the first of three Laklands I would eventually own. Made by a company in Chicago, it was a thing of beauty: a five-string with a natural light wood body, a maple neck, and a couple of Bartolini (the sonic equivalent of a BMW) soap bar pickups.

There was just one tiny problem—that bass had a thirty-five-inch neck, making it one inch longer than all the other bass guitars I'd ever played. That may seem like a trivial difference, yet, much like the Juzek upright I grappled with at DePaul, this bass was simply too big for my left hand. It sounded great; it looked fantastic; it was torturous to play.

Ultimately, I wised up, sold it, and bought a thirty-four-inch Sadowky five-string, which became my workhorse fretted bass. I played it, along with a kickass Lakland four-string fretless (also thirty-four inches), throughout the remainder of my career. Though they were fine instruments, I never became as intimately attached to the Sadowsky or the Lakland the way I'd been to the Mitchell Fender. After having been burned by that bass's loss I didn't want to open myself to that kind of heartbreak again.

You Wouldn't Know It to Hear Him

1985–1995

Q: What's the difference between a band and a bull?

A: A bull has horns up front and an asshole in the back.

<rim shot>

Leading a band is a high-anxiety occupation. Bandleaders put in long hours toiling behind the scenes: they schmooze events planners, cold call hotel food and beverage managers, meet with betrothed couples, and wear ruts in their office carpeting with anxious pacing, all of which leaves them little time to practice playing an instrument. Very few bandleaders have the skills to work as sidemen for other leaders, so their incomes are dependent on the work they generate themselves. Hence the carpet grooves.

A stereotypical bandleader is uptight, musically suspect, and kind of a jerk. This isn't true of all leaders but it is for too many to discount the general characterization. Sidemen need bandleaders to book the gigs and leaders need sidemen to play them. However, the symbiosis is an uneasy one, filled with mutual suspicion if not outright contempt.

I learned about this dynamic from the sideman point of view early in my career, but my understanding of it from the leader's perspective didn't coalesce until I started piloting my own jobbing band.

Around 1985, two good friends of mine, flutist Marc Perlish and pianist Kent Wehman, were in the same boat as I was, working primarily as sidemen. Kent booked a dozen or so gigs a year as a leader; Marc and I had nothing cooking to speak of. The three of us came up with the ostensibly brilliant idea to start our own live music company. If we had to play private parties to make ends meet, we reasoned, we might as well be the ones making *the big money* bandleaders earn.

"So … we'll all try to book as many leader dates as we can, right?" Kent asked.

"Yep. And on the nights when one of us isn't leading our own group, we can work for one another," Marc chimed in.

"Cool," I said.

That was a damn lie. I wasn't cool at all about any of this. My brief experience sub-leading a band for Mr. Gonif had left me feeling gun shy about the whole enterprise. Becoming an actual bandleader would mean putting myself out there in front of the band. No more making the low notes in the shadows next to the drummer. I'd be responsible for everything that happened before, during, and after the gig. I'd have to MC, call all the songs, manage the cats in the band, and be the "face" of the group. I'd also have to become a salesman, learn how to talk myself up to prospective clients as well as how to backslap caterers and glad-hand party planners. Nothing about any of that appealed to me in the least.

My monkey mind took off for the jungle canopy of anxiety.

Don't be stupid. You can't do this. You're not leader material. You like being a safe little sideman, with no responsibilities other than showing up with a bass. Don't waste your friends' time. Quit before you fuck it all up.

During rare moments of respite from this swinging through the brain trees, I reviewed the potential upsides of stepping into this new comfort-zone-smashing role:

- If I make more money per engagement I will have to work fewer of them.
- Fewer commercial jobs will allow more time for creative projects.
- I'll be able to choose the material—within reason. I'll still have to do "Brown Eyed Girl" and "Celebration," but maybe I can sneak in some Kinks or Talking Heads.
- I can hire my favorite musicians.
- More control, more money, more time for creative stuff, less crap music, less worry.

All well and good. On paper.

The timing, however, was atrocious. When Marc, Kent, and I joined forces, I was in the thick of a five-night-a-week jazz trio gig with Peter. I'd been hired to teach for the American Conservatory of

Music's jazz and commercial department. I got married in 1986 and would become a stay-at-home dad two years later, which coincided with our business revving up in earnest. The combination of these personal and professional commitments consumed big hunks of my time and energy, leaving little left over for creative projects—exactly what I'd hoped to prevent by making *the big money* as a bandleader.

The big money is another damn lie (like "softballs are soft"). When you sum up the investment of time and energy that goes into conferring with potential clients (including mothers-of-the-bride-from-hell), hiring musicians, hauling and setting up gear, maintaining a music library, leading the band, and playing your own instrument, the hourly rate comes out to about $1.27.

It was all too much. I descended into a deep funk, unlike anything I'd known previously. The pressure to succeed under these overwhelming circumstances reactivated the despair I'd faced immediately after I broke my finger fifteen years prior. I knew something had to be done to pull myself out of the doldrums, but I drew a blank on what that should be.

Someone suggested therapy.

Therapy? That's for crazy people. Or for losers who can't deal with their own stuff. Right?

I casually queried a few friends and family members and discovered that some of them were presently or had previously been in treatment with a mental health professional. And so, I set aside enough shame to make my way to a therapist's office for the first time. Though I didn't get much out of the work I did with this particular therapist, it put my feet on a path that would lead me to an entirely different life. But not yet.

About eight months after joining with Marc and Kent, I started to sing in self-defense. I certainly didn't need the additional complications, but the female vocalists in the biz at the time weren't covering some of the dude-centric pop music from the '60s and '70s. That music was the meat and potatoes of most jobbing bands' repertoire. Rather than hiring two singers, male and female, I decided I needed to sing some of that good old classic rock'n'roll myself. Here's a partial list of my, uh, lead vocal features: "Louie, Louie," "Gimme Some

Lovin'," "Old Time Rock and Roll," "Twist and Shout," "Jumpin' Jack Flash," "Margaritaville," and "I Heard It through the Grapevine."

Way back in my singing-along-with-show-tunes days, I'd clam up as soon as I sensed anyone might be listening. I was far too self-conscious to make a peep in front of other people. Now here I was, choosing to deliberately put myself in that same vulnerable position. *What the hell?*

I took lessons with Barb Noel, a wonderful singer and an uber-patient vocal coach. I practiced. I tried to sound like a real singer. I gradually overcame my abject fear of caterwauling in public. Real-life needs again pumped up my motivation and tamped down my inhibitions about being the center of attention as "the singer." The results were, shall we say, underwhelming. Pavarotti wasn't exactly quaking in his boots.

I had one glorious moment as a singer, however. My band had just finished a set at someone's wedding. I was sweating my ass off as I unstrapped my bass with one thought in mind: beer. I was about to exit when an attractive young woman came up to the edge of the stage.

"You have a beautiful voice," she said.

I started to laugh because I thought she must be pulling my leg. I'd just sung a brainless medley of "Twist and Shout," "La Bamba," and "Hang On Sloopy." She kept a straight face.

"No, I mean it," she insisted.

Is she hitting on me? Nah. Anyway, I'm very married.

"Oh, well . . . thanks!" I stepped off the bandstand shaking my head.

Lady, you have terrible taste.

My favorite story about my brief (some would say not brief enough) singing career was related to me by my regular coconspirator on the drums, Sarah. She told me she'd been shooting the breeze with a mutual friend and had mentioned that I sang a particular song on a gig. The friend said she didn't know that I sang. Without missing a beat, Sarah came out with "Well, you wouldn't know it to hear him."

Leading bands for five or so years taught me some things about building relationships, handling finances, and cajoling potential clients. I gleaned one additional lesson about myself, namely, that I should never sing in public.

To paraphrase Dr. McCoy, I'm a bass player, not a singer.

Jazz Man

1981–2002

> I take care of business and, every once in a while,
> I let 'em know it's me.
> —Christian McBride
> Jazz bassist extraordinaire

The second pillar of my musical life, after jobbing, was the one I cared most about, playing jazz. If I could have magically constructed the perfect life, I would have chosen to spend as many nights as possible on a bandstand playing jazz with the greatest musicians imaginable. I fantasized about moving to New York, where I'd work with world-class players at big-name jazz clubs like the Village Vanguard and the Blue Note. Or maybe I'd tour the country (hell, why not the world?) with some famous jazz artist. Such were the dreams of a twenty-something, too-big-for-his-britches bass player.

I didn't go to New York, but over a two-decade period, I did get the opportunity to perform with some heavy cats, including Clark Terry, James Moody, Bunky Green, Max Roach, Dizzy Gillespie, and, in a manner of speaking, Ray Charles. Some of these gigs were amazing; others not so much. Each of them made me a better musician in one way or another.

I worked with Clark Terry more than any other jazz star. He was a masterful player, but as I grew familiar with his style over several summers of jazz camp, his solos sounded more like practiced shtick and less like spontaneous improvisations. His playing, like his personality, struck me as jive—too slick, too-cool-for-school, and not especially interested in anyone else's input, musical or otherwise. Especially mine.

By my final June in Emporia, my relationship with Clark had deteriorated from tentative to troubled. He and I never recovered, musically or personally, from our rough first night playing together. I was frankly surprised that the camp director kept hiring me year after year.

It all finally came crashing down at the midpoint of one of the big band concerts, when the rhythm section normally played a tune as a quartet while the horn players rested their chops. This time, however, as the trumpets, trombones, and saxophones shuffled offstage, Clark snuck up behind me with the camp director and a young man I'd never seen before. This guy was apparently one of Clark's protégés. He'd come to sit in with the rhythm section—on bass. No one mentioned this beforehand. To make matters worse, Bob put me on the spot by saying, "He can use your bass, right?"

It wasn't a question.

I was flabbergasted that this was going down *in front of the audience*. What was I going to do—make a scene onstage? The fury and humiliation rose like bile in my throat.

Let me try to put this in context: there are unwritten rules of jazz etiquette concerning sitting in with a band. You're supposed to introduce yourself to the musicians, then politely ask if you can play a tune with them. If you want to sit in on a rhythm section instrument (piano, bass, or drums) you ask the player if it's OK with them, particularly if you're planning to use that musician's instrument.

Do I have to say that none of these protocols were followed? Clark and the camp director were all aware of them. What they did was deliberate and unconscionable.

I gave them both the sourest look I could muster as I handed my bass over to the Unknown Bass Player. When I complained to the camp director after the concert, he brushed me off with an offhand "Hey, man, it wasn't that big a deal." Not for him it wasn't.

The camp director neglected to invite me to return to Emporia the following summer. No surprise there. It would have been tough to say no—the camp was rewarding in lots of ways—but I like to think I'd have turned the gig down if he'd called me. I may have deserved a comeuppance, but in my mind, this public mortification in no way fit the "crime" of my youthful inexperience.

I'm sure of one thing, though: none of this would have happened if James Moody had been there that week. Clark was unable to appear at his eponymous camp one of those blazing summers in Emporia. Moody, a superb tenor saxophonist and flutist, played and taught in his absence, for which I'm eternally grateful.

He and I were simpatico right from the get-go. Our flights touched down at Kansas City International at about the same time, so we rode together in the van the camp had sent to cart us to Emporia. Moody was a personable and funny cat who seemed genuinely glad to hang out with me. During that ride to Emporia our conversation naturally turned to the subject of teaching music. The saxophonist told me he liked to start beginning students with the B-major scale. That's a key most young musicians dread because it has so many sharps (black keys on the piano).

"I start 'em in B; that way they'll never think it's any harder than any other key."

"Man, that's so wise."

I resolved to observe Moody closely during the week. I witnessed how careful and patient he was with students. His playing sounded fresh, even daring sometimes. At that age, I could already sense when a musician was "coasting," i.e., stringing together well-worn phrases from their bag of tricks, or truly pushing against their imaginative limits. Unlike C.T., I heard Moody play altogether different solos all week. He was the kind of musician I liked being around—warm, creative, encouraging, no nonsense. I was almost thirty years old when I discovered I wanted to be like James Moody when I grew up.

Another inspirational role model came into my life in the autumn of 1983: Bunky Green. Bunky was a light-skinned African American alto saxophonist. He carried himself like the brainy college professor he was; maybe five foot ten, slight of build with a head a bit too large for his body.

Bunky had forged his own jazz language, sounding to me like he'd welded together elements of Charlie Parker, Ornette Coleman, and Eric Dolphy. He taught for many years at Chicago State University, where he nurtured the talents of some great saxophonists like Steve Coleman, Greg Osby, and Rudresh Mahanthappa. It may have been his devotion to teaching that prevented Bunky from achieving the notoriety he deserved commensurate with his talent.

I met Bunky through drummer Jack, the same colleague who'd hooked me up with the Emporia jazz camp gig. I loved playing in this group, which also included pianist Ron Kubelik. Bunky's compositions were challenging yet satisfying to perform. He was generous with the space he provided for the rest of his quartet to contribute. Some jazz bandleaders rule with an iron fist, monopolizing all the solos, rarely doling out crumbs of time to their sidemen. I've played with a few of them. It's not fun.

In addition to his artistry as a composer and player, Bunky was an astute observer of musical ability. At a rehearsal one afternoon, he said to me, "Man, your playing is so solid. But it seems like you're still searching for your thing."

"Yeah, I guess so," I responded.

Bunky's remark knocked me down for a minute, until I realized how encouraging the man was being. His feedback was, in retrospect, right on the money, and he delivered it like the masterful teacher he was: one part compliment, one part constructive criticism. As the airline captain says while taxiing to the terminal, "We know you have a choice of airlines. Thanks for choosing ours." Bunky could have hired any bassist to play with his group. He chose me.

A few months into my association with him, Bunky invited me to perform and teach with his quartet at the Montreux Jazz Festival. It would be my first trip to Europe. I never thought I'd be financially able to travel overseas unless it was for a gig. Now, at the age of twenty-eight, I was doing exactly that. We were on our way to one of the most prestigious gatherings of musicians and audiences in the world.

Our quartet, plus Bunky's ever-present lovely wife, Edie, left O'Hare Airport for Switzerland in July 1984. We flew to Frankfurt, Germany, then trained down to our final destination. The day-long voyage to Montreux through the Alps was unspeakably picturesque. The city sits astride Lake Geneva, azure water to the west, pine-tinted mountains to the east and north. As a Midwestern flatlander, I gawked at the surroundings in awe.

We weren't there to sightsee, however. For four straight days, I taught master classes for bassists from all over Europe, some of whom spoke little English. Jazz is an international language, so I was able to communicate some concepts by demonstrating on the bass the festival had rented for me and by writing musical notation on the blackboard. When that wasn't enough, I solicited the aid of a couple of multilingual volunteers (plentiful in Switzerland) to help translate into Italian, French, Spanish, and German. I'd grown more comfortable doing group classes since my first week at jazz camp in Kansas three years prior. Unlike the camp kids, these were serious bass students, anxious to soak up whatever material I presented. As always happened when I taught, I learned more from them than they from me.

One surprising thing I learned from these students was that they thought I was a *somebody*. During our final class, I handed out a printed list of bass players for them to check out, including Paul Chambers, Charles Mingus, Ray Brown, Ron Carter, Dave Holland, and Scott LaFaro. One of the students smiled broadly at me and said, in a heavy French accent, "Why no Weelliam Harreeson?" Hot color rushed to my cheeks. The idea that any of these students would think I had any significance in the jazz world filled me with pleasure—and embarrassment. I knew my name had no place on a list of the most esteemed jazz bass players of all time. Still, it was gratifying to hear.

Early one evening, the Bunky Green Quartet performed at the Montreux Jazz Festival. Our band played not on the main stage but on one of the side stages outdoors. That didn't matter to me. I don't believe in any woo-woo crap about out-of-body experiences, but I can't describe how it felt with any other words when I ascended that stage.

There weren't a ton of people in the audience, but that didn't prevent me from imagining this moment as akin to Gary Karr's debut with the New York Philharmonic or Dave Holland's first gig with Miles.

This is it, man—what you've been aspiring to do. Now you're on your way.

I have no memory of what we played. I do recall playing a solo on some tune in D minor that elicited a short burst of applause. I imagine that my years of playing with Joe Daley helped me perform well under pressure. After our set, Bunky's group received a warm round of appreciation from the small assembly of listeners. I was as high as a NASA satellite.

I returned to Chicago with a renewed sense of confidence about myself as a musician. If I wasn't cut out for a career on the road with great jazz players, at least I felt stronger about my abilities as an accompanist and my creativity as a soloist. No one, including myself, could take away the reality that I'd gone to Montreux with Bunky Green and that we'd performed admirably.

My next chance to keep this momentum going came in April of 1985, when Max Roach came to the Midwest to play a concert at Governor's State University in the far south suburbs of Chicago. How I got the call to play this gig is a mystery. Maybe Bunky prodded Burgess Gardner (head of the jazz program at GSU) to give me a shout but I really don't know.

And don't care. All that mattered was that I was going to play a gig with Max Roach, who, like Moody and Terry, was one of the masters of modern jazz. He set the standard for bebop drumming in the '40s and '50s and played with many of the innovators of the music—Charlie Parker, Dizzy Gillespie, Bud Powell, Thelonious Monk, Charles Mingus, Clifford Brown, Miles Davis, and on and on. Mr. Roach had a reputation for being tough on sidemen, especially those he didn't know. As both the youngest and whitest member of this ensemble-to-be, I was a bucket of jumbled nerves when we all met for a rehearsal the day before the concert.

Tall, slender, Black, and soft spoken, Mr. Roach was often pictured wearing super cool sunglasses. He fought tirelessly against racism, both on and off the bandstand. His recording with vocalist Abbey Lincoln entitled "We Insist! Freedom Now Suite" exemplifies his lifelong commitment to racial justice. My brief encounter with him was a brush with real charisma and integrity, similar to the impression I had when I met Barack and Michelle Obama years later. Mr. Roach was a powerful man.

I have no recollection of the tunes we played. All I know is that Max Roach was an absolute pussycat with me, a real mensch. Playing with him was like putting on a pair of custom-made fur-lined gloves. His groove was that easy to slip into. He found ways to enhance what the other musicians were doing in each moment while still sounding entirely like himself. That's a tightrope that few musicians are able to consistently walk.

So you can imagine how astonished I was when Mr. Roach took me aside after the concert and said, "You make the quarter notes sing. Not everybody can do that."

I don't believe I've ever grinned any wider than I did right then. If only I could play with this man every night—that would have been a serious postgraduate bebop education. Alas, that would be the only time I had the privilege.

Privilege is the word that also comes to mind when I think of the night I got to play with jazz trumpeter Dizzy Gillespie. This one didn't go nearly as smoothly; it was much more of a "growth" experience.

Two summers before his death in 1993, Dizzy Gillespie toured with the Woody Herman Band. I was doing a few Midwest dates with the band around that time. One of those shows featured Mr. Gillespie, jazz icon and architect (with Charlie Parker and a few others) of modern jazz.

We rehearsed in the afternoon, breezing through a batch of arrangements without a hitch. The band was firing on all cylinders. Dizzy seemed pleased. Trouble ensued for yours truly when Dizzy called one of his big numbers, the Latin-flavored tune "Manteca." This song has a catchy mambo rhythm and an immediately recognizable bass line—one of those parts "everyone" knows. Everyone except me. "A Night in Tunisia," yes; "Manteca," for whatever reason, no. When he heard that I had no idea what I was doing with it, Mr. Gillespie did a 180 from the front of the stage and, looking rather bemused, sang the part to me. Though I was thoroughly abashed, I picked it up quickly and we played the rest of the arrangement without incident.

When "Manteca" rolled around during that evening's concert, I could feel a prickling anxiety rise. Drummer Bob Rummage launched into the song's iconic mambo groove. I froze. I couldn't for the life of me remember the bass part. After I missed my entrance sixteen bars later, Dizzy Gillespie, the most famous living jazz musician, had to walk upstage to the rhythm section and sing the bass line to me. *Again*. I prayed harder than I ever had in my life that the stage would open up and swallow me in its gaping maw.

What must Dizzy be thinking about me right now? I didn't want to know. In the courthouse of my mind, I threw the book at me. "Guilty as charged! Lock him up and throw away all twelve keys!"

Bob has never let me forget this blunder, because that's how musicians express affection for one another. I don't blame him. I'm also fairly certain that was my swan song with the Woody Herman Band. I truly hope I didn't hasten Mr. Gillespie's demise.

Meanwhile, I was having considerably more success with a roster of Chicago-based jazz artists. Two of the people I played many nights with, pianist Patricia Barber and guitarist Fareed Haque, gained some notoriety after my stints with them. (Their future popularity had nothing to do with me, one way or the other.) I performed with other fine musicians, like pianists Willie Pickens, Bradley Williams, Joe Vito, and Dennis Luxion, as well as violinist Johnny Frigo. I had the pleasure of playing with pianist/composer Fred Simon and Dave Onderdonk, a guitarist and composer, many times over the course of three-plus decades.

That these outstanding musicians would choose to hire me, again and again, meant more to me than playing one-nighters with their more celebrated kin. Each of their unique approaches to composing and performing propelled me toward becoming a more savvy, well-rounded, and flexible musician. I reflect on my time with them with great warmth and gratitude.

One result of the growth I experienced in the mid-to-late 1980s was the formation of my own jazz quintet. The group, made up of tenor sax, trumpet, guitar, bass, and drums, played mostly music I'd composed. We recorded an EP-length batch of tunes in 1989, most of which still sound fresh to my ears today. I used that recording to apply for a spot in the lineup for the 1990 Chicago Jazz Festival. We scored the gig and I brought the band to the festival in July.

Terry, Moody, Bunky, Max, Dizzy—my encounters with greatness weren't perfect by any means. Each experience brought new wisdom and new self-assurance. One important lesson I learned was that, in general, the better the musician, the nicer the person. It's not 100 percent accurate but it's true more often than not.

An instance of this adage came about as a result of a gig I played in late 2002. I rolled my bass into the University of Illinois at Chicago's Pavilion the morning of this performance. It was early; the stagehands were still setting up the platforms for our rehearsal. I sat down near the lone musician who'd arrived before me, a lovely looking woman holding what I took to be a viola case. We watched the guys put the finishing touches on the stage in silence. When they were done, I turned to my colleague and said, "It looks like it's safe to go on up there now."

"No it's not," she parried, with a mischievous look in her eye.

"Um, what do you mean?"

"You *are* a bass player, aren't you?"

It took a hot second for me to realize she was tease-flirting with me. We had a good laugh. I clambered onstage first, then made a show of gallantly "helping" her up the steps.

We were at the UIC Pavilion to prepare for a concert that evening with the man they called the Genius, Ray Charles. I wasn't there to play with Mr. Charles's rhythm section, as he traveled with his own guitarist, bassist, and drummer. My new friend and I were members of the string section for the orchestra accompanying the legendary pianist/singer.

The orchestra string parts were dull, mostly long notes, what musicians call "footballs," because the notation for half notes and whole notes looks something like the pigskin. That made no difference to me. Though Ray Charles was fifty feet away, sharing a stage with this legendary figure was momentous. In my mind, Mr. Charles's impact on soul and country music was analogous to Dizzy's influence on jazz.

I didn't get to meet the star. He was in Chicago to put on a show for an adoring audience and his "people" were very protective of their client. But, when the rehearsal ended, I introduced myself to Mr. Charles's electric bassist, a tall, slender white man with a long gray ponytail, who turned out to be Tom Fowler. I knew his name from some of Frank Zappa's LPs from the 1970s. Fowler is a great example of a musician's musician, someone who's well known among industry insiders but whose name audiences probably don't know.

"Tom, I noticed you doing something I'm not used to seeing with your right thumb. What's that about?"

"Oh, yeah, that's what I call the floating thumb. Instead of anchoring the tip of the thumb on the pick guard like most players do, I rest it across the strings. That way I can mute all the strings except the one I'm playing right that second."

"Wow, I never saw that before or thought to do it. Isn't it kinda awkward?"

"Well, y'know, like any other technique, it's weird until you get used to it. I do it completely unconsciously now."

"Makes sense. I'm gonna give it a try. Thanks for the lesson."

"No problem, my man. Good rapping with you."

Later that night, after returning home from an exhilarating evening backing up a legend, I grabbed a bass guitar and tried out the floating thumb. At first, I was all thumbs with it. After twenty minutes, though, the initial clumsiness gave way to a cleaner, more centered tone when I succeeded in muting the correct strings.

The floating thumb became an integral aspect of my electric bass technique in the ensuing months. I passed it along to dozens of students. That night at the UIC Pavilion was an unexpected turning point in my musical development. Thanks to Ray Charles for bringing together all the necessary ingredients. And thanks to Tom Fowler, for the new technique and for proving, once again, that the best musicians are the best people.

As had been the case with my Common Ground Quartet mentors and Joe Daley, I was in way over my head with these stellar musicians. It was nerve-racking to perform with artists who I knew could play circles around me. Most of them treated me like a creative partner even when I messed up. Their acceptance emboldened me to step out more visibly in the local jazz scene—composing and putting that quintet together, for example.

The balance I'd struck between commercial music and jazz may not have been ideal, yet during the '80s and '90s, I had at least one foot in the world of creative music, which was why I'd become a musician in the first place.

July, 1984

La Contrebasse Française

1984

By the autumn of 1984, I'd been playing double bass for fifteen years and had owned four instruments of various sizes and qualities. It was time to commit to a long-term relationship with one bass that fit my unique musical needs, chops, and body type. I was clear on what I *didn't* want in an instrument, but I couldn't have articulated what I *did* want. I figured I'd know it when I found it.

This was the predawn of the World Wide Web era. There was no Facebook or Instagram. I couldn't search for a bass on Google or eBay. Shopping for an instrument would be a laborious, methodical, time-consuming project. I was up for it.

I spent months auditioning as many basses as I could find at music stores and string shops in Chicago. Nothing felt quite right. So I decided to make a pilgrimage to New York City, the epicenter of American musical life. I'd be able to crash at my mother's apartment in suburban Jersey while I poked around the city for an instrument. I drove halfway across the country, determined to return with a sweetheart of a bass.

My first stop was Samuel Kolstein & Sons, a world-renowned string dealer located on Long Island. The place was set up like a Mercedes-Benz showroom, with a wide assortment of elegantly displayed instruments. I tried out some fine basses there, including the famous Prescott that had belonged to Scott LaFaro. The bass had been badly damaged in the car crash that claimed LaFaro's life in 1961 and then painstakingly pieced back together by the Kolstein staff. It wasn't for sale. I'm sure I couldn't have afforded it anyway, but it was a gas to play. I later learned that the Kolsteins donated it to the International Society of Bassists to be made available for loan to deserving young bassists, which was very cool of them. But none of

Kolstein's other basses knocked me out and their prices, in keeping with the classy vibe of the place, were sky high.

Next, I visited David Gage's shop in Lower Manhattan, which, in sharp contrast, felt more like a workshop than a showroom. Parts of instruments and woodworking tools were strewn about the place. I'd already test-driven dozens of basses in Chicago and at Kolstein's and was ready to be wowed by an instrument that stood out boldly from the crowd.

"Man, I broke my index finger playing softball a couple of years ago, so I need something that sounds great and plays easy," I told David. He thought for a moment.

"Hmm, I think I have something you might like." He steered me straightaway to a secluded corner of his shop.

As soon as I touched the neck of the bass he gently lifted off its stand, I had the oddest sensation that I already knew this instrument. It wasn't love at first sight, more like a rush of instantaneous familiarity. I spun the bass slowly around. Its varnish was dark orange with yellowish overtones. Gage hadn't yet told me anything about the bass, but its color, violin corners, and flat back whispered "Italian."

The bass seemed to glow with inner warmth, like some sort of relic. The back and ribs were adorned with jagged black lines etched into the wood at various depths. These markings reminded me of photographs I'd seen of the Martian canals. I'd come to find out that these striations were the unromantic remnants of worm damage.

I tentatively pulled an open string. A rich, complex vibration filled the shop. I met David's gaze for a long second. The shadow of a smile crossed his face.

"I'll leave you two alone," he said.

I brought the bass close to my body and placed all four fingers down on the A string. Out came an otherworldly sound, which I was able to produce with luxuriously little effort. I felt my pulse increase. I began testing notes for variations in tone quality in different registers of the bass. There were none. The instrument spoke with the same lovely voice in its high, mid, and low ranges. I grabbed a bow.

OK, but it probably doesn't sound nearly as good arco.

I was wrong. The bass sounded like the best dream ever, *pizzicato* and *arco*.

Every once in a while, David would pop by to see how we were getting along. My beatific grin told him everything he needed to know. I caught a glimpse of a nearby clock and realized I'd been playing this bass nonstop for over two hours.

Better put this thing down. Go take a walk, get some coffee, and clear your head.

When I returned, David showed me a few other basses for comparison, including one previously owned by legendary jazz bassist Ron Carter. A couple of these instruments were worth considering but I kept coming back to that mysterious orange bass.

The instrument turned out to be French, not Italian. It had a pedigree, official paperwork describing its origins and revealing some of its subsequent history. The bass was built in 1820 by M. Amelot, a luthier who toiled in obscurity during a period when a plethora of fine instruments were being made throughout Western Europe. Even Amelot's given name is an enigma. Here's the sum total of the information I've gathered about him:

> *Amelot (working life c. 1812–1845): Lorient, Brittany, France. Style of Lupot with red-orange varnish. Particularly fine double basses and 'cellos with rather good workmanship. Double basses much sought after and have realized high prices.*[1]

The Amelot bass lived in Europe until at least 1949, as evidenced by a label glued to the inside of the instrument's back that reads *"Certificat de Garantie."* It was placed there by Emile Francais, *luthier du Conservatoire National De Musique* on February 28, 1949. It's possible this bass played premiere performances of (then) contemporary music by Berlioz, Gounod, Offenbach, Massenet, or Saint-Saëns. How and why the bass crossed the Atlantic is a tantalizing unanswered question.

The instrument wound up in the hands of a man whose name I never learned, who performed with the Metropolitan Opera Orchestra. When he died, his widow put the bass up for sale on consignment at Gage's shop. According to David's records, the Amelot

---

1   The Dictionary of Violin and Bow Makers, Violin Research, Inc. https://www
.ricercare.com/research/library/references/dictionary1/frame.html

had been substantially restored sometime earlier by another well-known luthier, Lou DiLeone of New Haven, Connecticut, before making its way to the pit at the Met.

The prospect of owning a bass with such a rich backstory was enticing and unnerving. If I purchased it, the Amelot would be yet another bass that came into my life as a consequence of another musician's death. As I continued to put the instrument through its paces, a semi-famous jazz bassist named Harvie Swartz (now known as Harvie S) came in to confer with Gage about something. On his way out the door he hesitated for a moment, took a few steps in my direction, and looked me in the eye.

"Man," he told me, "you should buy that bass. You sound really good together."

I'd been at Gage's shop all day. Buying this instrument was going to be a huge decision, musically and financially, so I wanted to be as certain as possible before committing to the purchase. In some ineffable way, the Amelot had me in its thrall in those first few seconds, before I'd even played a note. But I needed those hours of concrete experience to quiet my anxieties. I wasn't being commitment-phobic, just careful.

The mechanics of the purchase, such as how I paid for it and what it was like driving it back to Chicago, are buried in some dusty corner of my brain. I do recall the purchase price and how I procured the dough. I still have the installment agreement I made with Bea, the mother of my ex-girlfriend Lindy. I paid her $225 on the fifteenth of the next sixty-five months at an interest rate of 12 percent per annum. Feel free to do the math if you're so inclined. Suffice it to say that, for me at that time, it was a *lot* of money.

I'd owned other precious things during my twenty-eight years on the planet but never something as special as this bass. Even the Mitchell Fender paled by comparison. It was way more to me than a "tool of the trade." Within a short time, the Amelot became integral to my musical personality, part of my signature sound, welded to my very soul. I guarded it with great care, as one would a child.

The bass was fragile and vulnerable to changes in the temperature and humidity. The wood was seasoned but still susceptible to either developing new cracks or having old ones reopen. I bought a humidifier. I was extra careful placing it in and removing it from my car. I always made sure there was plenty of space on all sides of us at gigs; I didn't want anyone getting close enough to do any damage.

My first engagement with the French bass was under the metaphorical baton of the infamous Georgia Frances Orchestra. That night we were performing in an immense ballroom at the Hyatt Regency Hotel. The gig was a fundraiser for George H. W. Bush, then a candidate for reelection as Ronald Reagan's running mate.

Everyone entering the ballroom had to submit to a thorough Secret Service security screening. I was "asked" to unpack my nearly two-hundred-year-old double bass in the classy confines of the hotel's loading dock. The SS officers shone their flashlights inside to confirm there were no hidden bombs or rocket launchers in there. When they were done poking and prodding me and my equipment, I rolled the rest of the way into the ballroom.

John and Georgia were already onstage, buzzing around with their anxiety levels maxed out. They'd hired a large ensemble for this job, one of the highest profile engagements they'd scored up to that point in their careers. We all felt the pressure pulsating outward from the two of them.

I pulled the padded black cover off the bass, rosined my bow, and began to tune up. As soon as I started tightening the D string, its tuning key broke off in my fingers. I stared at my left hand in disbelief.

"Really? You're doing this now, on our first gig together?"

The tuning mechanism had been custom made for this particular instrument using soft brass. I knew in that instant that it was going to be a helluva challenge to get that part repaired. But the immediate issue was: How was I going to get the bass in tune for this gig for the fucking vice president without a tuning key for one of the four strings?

I took a deep breath. Then I remembered that the bass was outfitted with a modern adjustable bridge, meaning that I could raise or lower the height of the strings (aka "the action"). Higher action equals higher pitch and vice versa. I nudged the bass in tune using this unorthodox method. Georgia and John didn't notice, so I assume it wasn't an issue for Mr. Bush either.

Musician friends, colleagues, and strangers were impressed by the tone we produced together. The bass recorded beautifully, so much so that audio engineers who'd "heard it all" would go out of their way to comment on it. I swelled with pride, as if I was personally responsible for the master craftsmanship that went into its construction. I'd usually mumble something like, "Thanks, I'm lucky to have it."

Other bassists were envious. One guy, a wheeler-dealer in basses and other gear, seemed offended that I'd purchased such a fine instrument.

"Yeah, man, that's the bass Marc Johnson had his eye on last time he was in New York."

The implication being that Marc, an excellent bassist who, like Scott LaFaro, played with Bill Evans, deserved the bass far more than I.

"If you ever decide to sell it, make sure to call me first."

Sure, dude, I'll do that.

When the bass suffered a mysterious shoulder injury around 2010, I brought it to master luthier Scott Henrie. Over the years, without me realizing it, the Amelot had acquired numerous nicks and bruises. Ancient repairs, never intended to be permanent, needed to be redone. The varnish needed retouching. Time and experience had worn the instrument down a bit, much like its owner. The Amelot needed a restoration and Scott was the right craftsman for the job. It took him eight weeks but he returned the bass to me in tip-top condition.

Now, nearly forty years later, the French bass leans comfortably in the corner of my office. Someday, probably in the not-too-distant future, I will find the bass a welcoming new home with a musician who'll appreciate it as much as I have. The bass deserves to be played more than the occasional few minutes I'm able to give it at this point. The year 2020 marked the instrument's two-hundredth birthday. The Amelot bass still glows with the same enigmatic aura as the day we met.

Amelot bass, built 1820

A Duck Among Penguins

1986

I'm onstage with my bass guitar, wearing musician's overalls (a tuxedo), shoehorned between keyboardist Dean Rolando and drummer Jim Widlowski. Our twelve-piece band, helmed by fellow DePaul alum Rich Daniels, is crowded onto a riser along one edge of a cavernous tent in Chicago's Grant Park. The gig is a black-tie fundraiser for who-knows-what charity. The venue is packed with politicos, corporate bigwigs, and their wives (plus a sprinkling of husbands), all decked out in their finest formalwear. The tuxes and dresses are black. The faces, including mine, are mostly white.

A commotion bubbles up near the main tent entrance. In strides an unexpected guest, Mayor Harold Washington.

"Well," begins the mayor. "I feel like a duck among penguins."

He's wearing a dark blue suit, not a tuxedo.

The mayor's quip could have been a metaphor for his political life in addition to a self-deprecating joke. Harold Washington was Chicago's first African American mayor. He was relentlessly opposed by the infamous majority-white city council, led by two evil Eddies, Vrdolyak and Burke. During Washington's first stormy term in office, these "Council Wars" (as they were dubbed by the local media) prevented him from enacting most of his legislative agenda, much the same way an obstructionist Congress would later inhibit progress throughout the presidency of another fine Black Chicagoan.

At this point in my career as a freelance bassist, most of the people I worked for and with were white men. A person of color might make an occasional appearance but, unfailingly, if the gig was downtown or farther north, mostly white musicians played for mostly white audiences. Black musicians worked the South Side, reflecting the intractable racial divide in Chicago. And, with rare exceptions, women who didn't sing, regardless of race, weren't welcome in any musical group.

The idea that my peers and I were perpetuating systemic racism would never have occurred to us at the time. I saw that Black and Brown musicians, including some I knew from the jazz scene, weren't getting hired for those lucrative downtown gigs, but I did nothing about it. Musicians of color were invisible to white contractors and bandleaders.

It was another iteration of the same old American story: without acknowledging rampant structural racism and sexism, and exerting conscious effort to achieve racial and gender diversity, proportional representation in the music business was never going to happen.

Our union's history reflects this bifurcated racial inequality. The Chicago Federation of Musicians' designation is Local 10-208. The hyphenation is the result of segregation. When the precursor to the modern union, Local 10, was organized in 1901, it barred African Americans from membership. Black musicians responded by forming their own union, Local 208. The two groups didn't merge until 1966. I've talked with colleagues, both Black and white, about this over the years. It seemed that most musicians were either ignorant of this history or preferred to forget it.

Half a century later, Chicago's musical community remained stubbornly separate and unequal. In the '80s and '90s, I felt wedged in the middle of an insoluble moral dilemma: working to expand the pool of players to include more people of color would have begun to even the playing field between Black and white musicians—*and* it would have inevitably made it less likely I'd get called for certain gigs. It wasn't in my best interest to advocate for inclusion.

I knew a certain Black bass player—I'll call him Lawrence. Based on his talent and skill set, he ought to have been getting hired for musical theater jobs, some of the best-paying steady work in the music biz. Lawrence exuded a calmness that reflected his years of experience in recording studios and with touring bands. But theater contractors who booked those shows hadn't worked with him, so he didn't get the opportunities. I could have introduced Lawrence to the right people, but I was too worried about my own position in the musicians' pecking order to stick my neck out for him. The cognitive dissonance between what I knew was the right thing to do and what I was willing to risk precipitated a storm of crushing guilt whenever I gave these thoughts any mental bandwidth. So, I did what I imagine many of my white musician peers did: I tried not to think about it.

Early one morning not long after that charity ball, I was scoping out a parking space near a South Side elementary school. I was scheduled to meet up with jazz pianist Willie Pickens and the rest of his quartet. We were about to play a concert and do a Q&A for the students, faculty, and staff.

Willie spotted me and waved me over to the parking lot. He was a stocky man in his fifties with a welcoming grin. One of a handful of Black musicians I'd gotten to know and make music with regularly, we had taught and played concerts together at the American Conservatory of Music and elsewhere.

The pianist introduced me to the tenor saxophonist and the drummer, guys I'd never met. I was the only white dude in the band. I knew I was good with Willie—he'd hired me, after all—but I wondered if these other musicians were going to be cool with me. Anxiety stirred in my belly as we were escorted into the auditorium, gear in tow. I stuffed down the jitters as best I could; I didn't want these cats to think I couldn't cut it.

Onstage, I peeled the cover off my double bass and set the instrument down on the polished oak floor. Students filed in, row by row, classroom by classroom. The auditorium filled with children and teachers. It was surprisingly quiet. The kids were watching us, mesmerized by the sight of us setting up our instruments.

All at once, a panic arose in my throat. Besides me, there wasn't a single white person in the room. My face burned. My hands turned clammy. I scanned the room frantically, searching for someone, anyone, who looked at all like me. *No. I'm alone.* I suppressed a visceral urge to grab my bass and make a run for the exit. *What am I doing here, with these musicians, on this stage, with these people? Who the hell do I think I am?* It was all I could do to stay put. I forced myself to freeze, still as a mannequin.

At that moment, a gig from last summer hijacked my thoughts. That day, I performed at an outdoor festival in front of several hundred people in Stone Park, a tiny Italian American enclave west of Chicago. I was completely at ease that cool sunny afternoon, playing with two other white men and Frankie Donaldson, an African American drummer. Not a single Black face in that ocean of onlookers. I turned to Frankie, a longtime colleague and friend, and asked him what he made of this.

"Makes no difference to me," he said with a shrug.

"Isn't it off-putting?"

"Maybe the first hundred times. I had to get used to it to survive in this fucked up-world."

The present snapped back into focus. I was definitely *not* used to this.

The kids were on their best behavior, sitting there watching us intently. The other band members were chatting amiably while I was paralyzed by irrational fear, *of what?* Was I even going to be able to play in that state? I bit my tongue and picked up the bass.

"Let's hit with 'Billie's Bounce,'" Willie called across the stage. He snapped his fingers on beats two and four. "One . . . two . . . one, two, three, four."

My body knew what to do with this twelve-bar blues. I fixed my gaze on the drummer's right hand as I matched the boom of my walking bass line to the ting of his ride cymbal. The tenor player blew like Sonny Rollins as he weaved Bird's melody through Willie's crisp accompaniment. As ever, the music took over.

The kids broke out in enthusiastic applause after every number. During our postconcert Q&A, one little girl asked me, "How old is your cello?"

I'd calmed down enough by then to answer with ease. "Well, this isn't a cello. This is called a double bass. It's much bigger than a cello and has a deeper tone. This bass was built in 1820, so it's almost two hundred years old."

I smiled as I heard a few people *ooh* and *ahh*. I almost felt as if I belonged.

In the 2010s, I observed some positive developments in Chicago's music scene. More women and people of color were showing up regularly on symphonic stages, in orchestra pits, and in dance bands at private parties all over the city and suburbs. The band for the three-plus-year run of *Hamilton* was integrated by race and gender. And, until the pandemic wiped out everything, I was glad to see that Lawrence was in the bass chair at some of the better-paying theater pits around town.

Yet there's plenty more work to be done, in Chicago and the rest of the country. If we don't incinerate ourselves, and if the country doesn't tear itself apart at its political seams, perhaps there will come a time when no one is made to feel isolated from the flock of humankind.

At the Lakeside Green

"**P**ick a key, any key," says Peter from his post at the grand piano. "How 'bout D-flat?"

"OK, good one."

Peter starts meandering through some standard tune *rubato* (out of time), one that's usually rendered in a more pedestrian key such as C or F or B♭. When he gets to the top of the second chorus, he sets up a tempo and Rick and I join in.

We're playing the Twelve-Key Game, which our jazz trio uses to shake ourselves out of the doldrums. It's on-the-job ear training, a way to practice transposing on the fly. When you play five hours a night, five nights a week, for three and a half years, you have to find ways to maintain your energy—and sanity. We change keys, tempos, meters (swapping 4/4 for 3/4 or vice versa), and styles (a swing tune becomes a samba, for instance); anything to prevent us from getting into too much of a rut.

The setting for a thousand nights of this is the Lakeside Green, a tony bar on the ground floor of the Chicago Hilton and Towers Hotel. The three of us are set up on an imposing faux-marble stage in front of luxurious armchairs and knee-high two-tops. Plate glass windows expose us to the sidewalks of Michigan Avenue and Balbo Street. A mezzanine hangs twelve feet over our heads. On nights when there's a party in the ballroom up there, we can feel the thump-thump-thump-thump of a DJ.

We worked at the Lakeside Green Sundays through Thursdays, which left us available for other gigs on Fridays and Saturdays. I organized every day around the moment I had to jump into my tuxedo, load my gear (upright bass, amp, and gig bag) into my Subaru station wagon, and drive downtown. This was a boon for my checking account but meant that I often went for months on end without a day off. When my then wife returned to work after my son's birth, I became his primary caretaker, which, while wonderful in many ways, led to the acute curtailment of my sleeping hours. It wore me down.

I wasn't the only member of the trio who suffered from unrelenting fatigue. One night, after having played solo piano for three hours, then with the trio for another four, Peter momentarily nodded off *in the middle of a song*. Suddenly, the notes he was playing sounded like gobbledygook. I looked over at him just as his head jerked upright. It was pretty damn funny. We got a lot of future mileage out of "you remember that time you fell asleep while you were playing?"

The ribbing came my way too, of course. One time when I came to work not feeling my best, I was compelled to put my bass down in the middle of a tune and run to the bathroom. When I eventually returned, a pound lighter and several shades paler, Peter asked, "Was it something I played?"

It was during this gig that Peter and I developed the musical rapport that would characterize our partnership from then on. We built a huge repertoire and, with Rick's assistance, created unique arrangements of many of the tunes on the bandstand. "Arrangements While You Wait" is the oft-used phrase for this. We weren't always at the top of our game, especially in the final hour or so at the end of our work week. But when we were on, we were *on*.

Here's an example of how tuned in Peter and I were to one another. We were in a recording studio, in the middle of a take of Leonard Bernstein's haunting ballad "Some Other Time." The first chord of Peter's solo chorus was C major seventh. The rules of harmony indicate that I should play a C at the beginning of that measure. Instead, I played a G♯, a pitch that would have sounded completely wrong had Peter not chosen to play the chord as a C major seventh with an augmented fifth (the altered note is a G♯). How did I know he was going to do that? I didn't. I just made an educated guess that he might go there—and he did. Weird. But that kind of stuff happened regularly; that's how well we knew each other's playing.

Playing music, especially jazz, for so many hours together leads to a kind of intimacy that's unlike any other. It was akin to—and this is going to sound strange—*un mariage jazz à trois*. Each of us paid close attention to the subtle details of the others' playing, as if we were breathing together. Maintaining this kind of attunement requires concentrated energy and a willingness to be open to the contributions of each player. At its best, our band had that special bond.

On the other hand, there was always friction regarding rhythm.

Part of my job description as a bass player in any situation was to maintain a steady pulse. Ideally, this is everyone's responsibility, but in real life it often falls to the bassist and drummer (if there's one on the gig) to keep the band's tempo in check. Humans aren't metronomes. They have tendencies, either to speed up (rush), to slow down (drag), or to do some unpredictable combination of both (what I call Russian Dragon).

Regulating tempos has to be done cautiously because tempo wars can fray tempers. There were times when I had to chomp on my tongue to prevent myself from potentially offending someone by pointing out that the band was galloping ahead because they were pushing the tempo so hard. It's not something anyone wants to hear. Or admit. Having a good sense of time is a matter of pride; it's a skill musicians work on and strive to perfect. To be told your time is messed up is like being told you're a failure. Not cool at all.

Of course, I've been on the receiving end of this unwelcome criticism. An especially awkward situation arose when I was playing with Ron, a pianist well known for his talent and his less-than-exemplary social skills. We were performing as a trio with a trumpet player in a venue with awful reverberant acoustics. Something shifted with the pulse when we arrived at the bridge of a ballad, I can't recall what exactly. Ron whipped around on the piano bench and flashed me a nasty sneer.

"Quit dragging," he snarled.

Gulp. Please take me now, Lord.

The next day I practiced for an hour with a metronome to reassure myself that my time did not, in fact, suck.

Bass players are at a sonic disadvantage to pianists. The sheer density of sound a keyboard player is able to produce can easily obliterate a bass line. A pianist has ten fingers, which they can deploy simultaneously. I have four left-hand fingers and two on the right, and I can generally only spit out one note at a time. The acoustic odds are therefore not in my favor. It's challenging to be assertive, especially if you're trying to be surreptitious, when you're so outgunned by the volume of your frenemy. The presence of a sympathetic drummer increases the likelihood of success controlling the tempo, because drummers can make a racket when they want to. We have a lot more power working in tandem.

To be blunt, our Hilton trio had problems with rushing. Peter knew he had difficulty reining in his enthusiasm, but I don't believe he ever realized the effort it sometimes required for me and various drummers to hold back his horses.

One of the times I failed to do this occurred during another recording session. I'd booked a quintet, consisting of flute, vibes, piano, bass, and drums, to record three or four of my compositions. During the first take of one of the tunes, things were swinging along nicely when, after a marvelous flute solo by my pal Marc, Peter got so carried away during his chorus that he wound up a full beat and a half ahead of the rest of the band. We had to abort the take, much to Marc's dismay and Peter's chagrin.

There's another, even trickier, layer of complexity in the mix. More times than not, the piano player in a duo or trio is the boss. He or she does the hiring, leads the gig, and writes the checks. You've been hired presumably because the pianist likes your playing, likes you, or ran out of other bass players to call on a busy night. Either way, part of your agenda is to encourage this person to hire you again. You don't want to do or say anything antagonizing.

During our residency at the Hilton, I began to see how the latter complication was playing out between Peter and me. He had booked this steady job and hired me to do it. In fact, 98 percent of the time, at the hotel and on jobbing gigs, he was the boss and I was a sideman. Yet, outside of work we acted as if we were the best of pals. We never addressed this underlying hierarchy, which lurked unacknowledged and unspoken for decades. Over time, I learned to be wary, never sure whether we were relating as equals or in the context of the implicit inequality of our business roles. This uncertainty confused and rankled me, but I was too cowardly to bring it up with Peter directly.

Three and a half years after we started working at the hotel, Hilton management decided they wanted to "go a different direction" (which is corporate-speak for "you're fired"). Peter sweet-talked them into auditioning a more pop-oriented quartet he assembled. He plopped a synthesizer atop the piano, hired his guitarist buddy Frank, an electric bassist named Mark, and Steve, a drummer. The hotel didn't dictate what musicians he could use but Peter decided the band needed a "different look" to convince the hotel they were buying a whole new "product."

I thought this was bullshit. By then I was a more than adequate bass guitarist and could have easily adapted to the new aesthetic. As far as I was concerned, this was an arbitrary and wholly unnecessary decision.

"It's just business," my friend told me, which sounded like a line one guy might say to another in a Mafia movie right before he pulls the trigger.

Maybe Peter was right and his quartet wouldn't have secured the gig if I'd shown up with them. We'll never know. But the bitter tang of resentment hung over our relationship for some time after this.

There would be other disappointments and conflict in years to come. But Peter and I also helped each other through difficult times, had a lot of laughs, and made some good music together. In October of '01, after two decades of playing with one another under conditions ranging from ideal to ridiculous, we produced our one and only duo album, *Mood Swings*.

Peter and I went into the studio with our friend Jim Massoth in the control room to record whatever tunes we felt like playing as the day progressed. We had a vast shared repertoire and a mutual desire to treat the recording session as if we were playing an ordinary duo gig—like so many we'd played in the past. The eclectic track list included music by Cole Porter, Chick Corea, Graham Nash, and Benny Golson. We also did one of Peter's tunes. We played one take of each song. If we botched it we moved on to the next one without a backward glance. We took our time, *kibbitzed* between takes, and had a lot of fun. There are no edits or fixes of any kind on the finished album, which was a matter of pride for both of us.

Mood Swings is a loving, authentic musical portrait of the rich relationship Peter and I forged over a long stretch of our lives.

The Hilton Trio: Bill, Rick, and Peter, c. 1987

Mr. Holland's Lesson

1976/1987

" **W**hat was it like when you parted ways with Chick to form your own band?"

"Well, Chick Corea had booked a recording date with me and Barry (Altschul) for ECM, which we thought was going to be an extension of the music we'd been playing with Circle," Dave tells me, leaning closer to the microphone. "Imagine our disappointment when he brought in a bunch of bossa novas."

"Wow, yeah."

"It was clear that we were headed in different directions, kind of like when I left Miles's band in 1970, y'know?"

"I can imagine."

No, I couldn't. Not really. I'm sitting in Dave Holland's hotel room recording an interview with him for my radio show on WNUR. It's 1976; I'm nineteen. This moment is a fantasy come true. I'd been *plotzing* to have a chance to talk one-on-one with my bass hero since the end of high school. Now he's right here in front of me, sipping a cup of tea, and answering questions I toss his way.

What I really wanted was a bass lesson from Dave, the one I didn't arrange with him during the Creative Music Workshop. I settled for doing this interview, not because he said no to a lesson but because I was too chicken-shit to ask for anything more at the time.

The decade of the '80s was jam-packed with work and the period of my greatest ambition as a musician. I studied with bassist Mark Kraemer and cellist Karl Fruh to help fill in some of the *teshnical* gaps left over from my work with Mr. Benfield. I took piano lessons from Goldie Golub at Roosevelt University. A bit later I had a few sessions with a strict sourpuss of a violin instructor named Mr. Ghertovici. At DePaul I took jazz harmony and arranging classes.

However, I'd never had the opportunity to study with a jazz bass player. Everything I knew about playing improvised music I'd learned by listening to recordings and playing with more experienced musicians.

So when Dave Holland brought his quintet to Chicago's Jazz Showcase for a week in the spring of 1987, I was determined to get the lesson I was too scared to ask for the previous times we'd met. One night between sets at the Showcase I mustered the courage to speak with him about spending an hour as a student with him. Much to my great surprise, his immediate answer was, "Yeah sure. When do you want to get together?"

It was a chilly Saturday afternoon, April 18, when I wheeled my bass up to Dave's room in the Blackstone Hotel, located directly across Balbo Street from the Hilton where I was playing with Peter and Rick. Dave was well proportioned to be a bass player; much better than I. He was tall and slender, with close-cropped brown hair, a well-trimmed beard, long arms, and expressive fingers. His handshake was surprisingly gentle.

There was a cup of tea and a book of poems by Dylan Thomas on Dave's night table. He also had a music stand with a copy of "A Contemporary Concept of Bowing Technique for the Double Bass" by Frederick Zimmermann open to what looked like a well-worn page.

"What do you use the Zimmerman book for?" I asked, after greetings and unpacking of basses.

"Yeah, I know it's written for orchestral bass players, but I use it to develop evenness of tone between first and second fingers playing *pizzicato*."

I'd struggled with this book with Mr. Benfield and knew how fiendish some of the exercises were.

"That must be, uh, challenging."

"It's a workout, for sure. As long as you bring it up, why don't I show you how I apply the book to my practice regimen?"

"OK, sure." I was up for whatever Dave had to offer.

Dave spent a generous ninety minutes with me. He demonstrated exercises for both left and right hands. Then we played some duets, including an exhaustive reading of Scott LaFaro's challenging tune "Gloria's Step." Dave had nice things to say about my Amelot bass and made some suggestions on how I could further improve my attack and tone.

"I've got a five-nighter right across the street in the Hilton hotel," I made sure to tell him, with the unspoken hope that he might stop by between his band's sets to check out our trio.

"You can get a lot of stuff together on a gig like that," he said.

Dave reinforced the concept I'd been trying to put into practice for several years—that a person (in this case, me) will never be able to overpower the bass.

"You have to be strong yet supple to get your sound out. And you have to use just enough energy to propel the music forward without running out of stamina before the set ends. It's tricky. And don't forget: practicing and playing are two very different things."

Dave went on to explain that the former is the time to pay attention to all the physical and intellectual details of the skills you're trying to cultivate. When you're on the bandstand, however, forget about all of that and play from your heart and intuition.

Toward the end of our meeting Dave told me, "You're a no-bullshit musician. I like that." I cherish that remark to this day.

We hadn't discussed payment before our meeting. nor did he ask for any money when we were about to part. I'd brought fifty bucks with me and offered it to him on my way out the door.

"I can't say no," Dave said, as he graciously accepted the cash. The time we'd spent together was well worth the thirteen-year wait.

Soon after we met for this lesson I read that Dave would be the artistic head of a two-week intensive jazz training program the following summer in Banff, Canada. The faculty was going to include some of the most well-respected creative musicians of that era. It sounded like a contemporary version of the Creative Music Workshop.

I wanted to go, but in early 1988 my wife became pregnant with our first child. Her due date was mid-August, right smack in the middle of that fortnight in Banff. So I stayed put, played my gigs, took care of my wife, and was privileged to witness the birth of my son. I'd like to think Dave would have approved of my choice.

From the Far East to the Wild West

1995–1998

Malcolm Ruhl ushered me into one of the performance spaces at Victory Gardens Theater. He and I had met when he hired me to sub for him on a wonderful little show called *Woody Guthrie's American Song* in early 1994. Malcolm is a diminutive man with a serious but mellow demeanor. He plays a bunch of instruments, including bass, all of them well. He'd been hired to music direct *Song of Singapore*, a show that was about to have its Chicago premiere. I was there to audition for it. As he put me through my paces ("Play a walking bass line on an F blues," "Improvise on an A-minor seventh chord," "Sight-read this part"), a bemused smile materialized on Malcolm's face. I guess he thought I was good enough to play the show.

Song of Singapore is a musical set in 1941, just prior to the Japanese invasion of that Southeast Asian island. The show had been a minor hit in New York City; the producers were hoping to replicate that success here in Chicago. They spent a fortune converting a vacant space in Piper's Alley (the same building that houses the Second City comedy club) into a 1940s-era dance hall. The show was to be an immersive theater experience that would include an Asian-style restaurant and a bar serving drinks with goofy names like "The Taiwanon" and "The Frank Sumatra."

I played Taqsim Arco, bassist for the Malayan Melody Makers, the house band at Freddy's Song of Singapore Café. We were onstage for the entire show and thus had to be in costume and in "character" for the duration. I didn't have any lines but I did have a crucial bit of stage business, which I cannot reveal for fear of spoiling the plot if you ever happen to see this show. My advice, however, would be to avoid doing that.

It was booked as an open run, but *Song of Singapore* went gentle into that good night after about three months because . . . well, because it's an awful show. It has a preposterous plot with racist overtones (which didn't register with me at the time) and a merely adequate score. Paul Slade Smith, a cast member who went on to do some impressive big-time work (touring with *Wicked* and working on Broadway) dubbed the show *Songs We'll Sing No More.*

I was disappointed that *SoS* was so lousy and that the run ended so soon. However, I was pleasantly surprised by the kick I got from being onstage instead of under it for a change. The guys in the dressing room, actors and musicians, had a blast together. I hadn't felt this kind of camaraderie outside of a jazz club for as long as I could remember.

Playing Taqsim was taxing, physically and mentally, for shockingly low pay, even with a union contract. The producers, having lavished a bundle of cash on the physical environs, were parsimonious with their labor force. I had to fight for a reduced-rate parking spot in the attached lot, as there was no safe place to store my bass overnight. A few weeks into the run, the producers whittled the menu down to three items. We knew it was only a matter of time before we'd all be at liberty.

My character's name was a sly joke but my castmate Luke Nelson had the best moniker from *Song of Singapore*, Spike Spaldeen. Luke was too young and Midwestern to understand the meaning of the name. Having been raised in New York City, I knew that a "spaldeen" was the pink rubber sphere we used for stoop ball, stick ball, hand ball, wall ball, "out," and whatever other baseball-like games we dreamed up in the 1960s. The ball was stamped with the word "Spalding," but kids from the boroughs knew how to pronounce it the *right* way.

Meeting Luke was the primary benefit of playing *Song of Singapore*, because he subsequently invited me to play *Always, Patsy Cline*, a gig that would go for about a year and have a lasting impact on my future.

Always, Patsy Cline played the Apollo Theater (just up the street from my DePaul-era digs) from January through October of 1997, later moving to Victory Gardens Theater for its final five months. This production featured local superstar Hollis Resnik as Patsy. I had the good fortune to perform with Hollis in one of her first leading roles, Kim in *Bye Bye Birdie*, way back in 1981. I didn't actually meet her then; I was too shy to introduce myself to the show's star ingenue. It was a little easier sixteen years later.

Patsy's band was onstage for the whole show. The costume designer dressed us in black jeans with cowboy boots, long-sleeved black shirts with white flowery appliqué up near the pockets, and, of course, black Stetsons. We looked ridiculous.

At the top of each show, the Bodacious Bobcats (our band's name) played "Walkin' after Midnight" with Patsy. As the applause faded, my job was to set down the bass, walk to center stage, grab the old-timey microphone on its stand, and strike it into the shadows of stage left. I executed this move without mishap a hundred times until, one night, I caught the heel of one of my clunky boots on the mike cable as I was returning upstage to my bass. Somehow, I managed not to fall—but it was close. After the show, Sarah Underwood, the actress playing Patsy's friend Louise told me, "Dude, I saw you almost go down. If you'd fallen I would've had to deal with it. Glad you didn't."

Me too, sister, me too.

The high point of each show for me was the moment when I got to deliver a line to Louise in a thick Texas drawl: "There ain't no way."

My kids, ages ten, seven, and six, got to see me onstage in cowboy garb several times and learned to sing the songs from the show. Friends and relatives came to see it too, which was always gratifying. We even had visits from a few celebrities.

One night, Melissa Manchester attended a show, which caused quite a buzz backstage. It was a sold-out performance, which usually meant there'd be welcome laughs and applause at appropriate times. Near the end of the show, Patsy sang a few numbers without interruption by scenes, often a high point for audiences. We arrived at that juncture and, for the first time ever, the cable for my bass guitar shorted out, emitting a teeth-chattering bzzzzzz until the sound engineer muted the bass in the theater's PA system.

Sheesh, why me?

Ms. Manchester visited us backstage and was very complimentary, until she turned to me and said, "Too bad about that buzz from your guitar. I was wondering why you didn't just grab the doghouse."

A sheepish shrug accompanied by a shit-eating grin was all I could manage in response.

Always, Patsy Cline ran for approximately four hundred performances. I stayed through the end of November, quit, then agreed to play the last month in February 1998. All told, I played well over three hundred shows.

The combined stage time I collected playing *Woody Guthrie's American Song*, *Song of Singapore*, and *Always, Patsy Cline* planted the seedling of desire to do more—I didn't yet know what—in the theater.

Cast and crew of *Always, Patsy Cline*, 1997

The Other Side of the Footlights

"Wow, great breasts," I exclaimed.

"Wow, great breasts," she deadpanned, taking a small step backward.

"Wow, gr-r-reat breasts," I growled, eliciting nervous titters from the other students.

"Wow, great breasts." She crossed her arms over her chest and turned scarlet.

"You're embarrassed," I said, softer now.

"I'm embarrassed." She looked at the floor.

"You're embarrassed." I looked away.

"*You're* embarrassed!" she called out.

"I'm embarrassed," I said, my eyes filling.

Thus began one of my first improvised "Repetition" exercises in class with the late acting instructor Victor D'Altorio. He shepherded me and an earnest bunch of nervous neophytes through Sanford Meisner's acting method, in which this exercise plays a central role. It was the fall of 1996; I was forty years old and hadn't been anywhere near a stage without a bass in my hands since high school.

So why then? What drove my newly rekindled desire to show up in front of the footlights instead of remaining in the dark behind them, as I'd been content to do for so long?

Sure, I'd grown more comfortable appearing onstage as a musician. Acting, not playing the bass, would be an entirely different kettle of fish. In journal entries I made at the time I noted a shift in attitude about playing gigs. I was becoming "lackadaisical" about my freelance jobs. It had been a long time "since I thought of my non-theater gigs as performances." They'd become ho-hum, "just another thing to get through." It was as if I'd fallen asleep, musically and emotionally.

In response, I was becoming restless. Dissatisfied. Bored and boring. Playing music, most of it commercial, wasn't meaning much to me anymore—and hadn't for some time. Showing up and making the low notes had lost its zing.

This somnambulism was the impetus for seeking out Julia Cameron's workbook *The Artist's Way*. The exercises in that book hit home hard. The most telling of them were fill-in-the-blank phrases, one of which spoke to me loud and clear: "If I weren't so afraid, I'd _____." Time and again my answer was "be an actor."

One day my inner voice yelled, *Fuck it, what are you waiting for? Make some calls and see if there's an acting class that sounds right for you.*

It was time to wake up and smell the fear. So I signed up for the Meisner training with Victor.

Victor D'Altorio and I were about the same vintage. We'd both gone to Northwestern in the early '70s. That's where the similarities ended. Victor was gay, about six foot two, with a closely shaven head and a couple days' sandpaper growth on his face. He went to the gym at least five days a week, and it showed. There was no doubting his Italian heritage either, from his swarthy skin tone to his brash manner. He would have killed as one of the Corleones in a *Godfather* movie.

Victor's voice cut right through you—loud, pointed, nasal—and made it clear that he had no tolerance for bullshit. He had an uncannily large mouth, which flapped open and closed cartoonishly when he spoke.

Here's what he told us the first day of class:

"I'm a *ho-mo-sexual*. I like to have sex with men, ya got it? Some of you look like you've led pretty sheltered lives and probably haven't met someone as direct as me about their sexuality. This is who I am—a gay man. Be clear with who you are, and you'll do fine in this class."

Mm, OK.

I liked him. And he scared the crap out of me.

My involvement with drama dated back to middle school, a time when I was an anxious, dorky, bashful preadolescent. I knew how to disappear into the woodwork when I felt the least bit nervous, which was often. I also knew how to make people laugh and loved the feeling of power that talent gave me. An internal ping-pong match between these conflicting impulses, toward shyness on the one hand and the desire to stand out in a crowd on the other, played out in an unending rally through much of my youth.

During the two summers between sixth and eighth grades, my parents sent me to Beginner's Showcase, a drama camp/summer stock theater in tiny Georges Mills, New Hampshire. Years later, my mother told me she was worried I was becoming antisocial and had thought this camp might help me break out of my shell.

I chose the radio/TV/film major because the curriculum was right in the wheelhouse of my main non-musical interests at the time. It also sounded ideal for an introvert like me. I drifted toward drama only when it became obvious that the camp's R/T/F department was more fiction than reality.

The first day of camp Phil (my friend from Tenafly), Wayne, and I—three forlorn film nerds—stood outside the whitewashed wooden door marked "TV/Film Studio." No one opened the door when we knocked so, we trooped over to the main office in search of answers.

Bob, the doughy middle-aged camp codirector (who was rumored to have been the original Ronald McDonald), seemed flustered by our presence.

"Why don't you boys head over to the tent," he lisped. "Mr. Romano is teaching a beginning acting class which I'm sure you'd find interesting."

Three pairs of eyes rolled in unison.

"Well, I don't know why Tom isn't here," said Bob, arms akimbo. Tom, we'd soon learn, was the Top 40 disc jockey from WKBR ("The Big K") in Manchester who'd been hired to teach us the ins and outs of radio and TV.

"Just go on over to the tent and I'll keep you posted."

We retreated from the office and bivouacked in a semi-circle to contemplate our next move. Wayne and Phil were not the least bit game to check out the class.

"I'm gonna go back to sleep," Phil declared. "Wake me up if any-thing happens."

Wayne wandered off somewhere as well. I shuffled toward the tent. I didn't have an interest in acting *per se*. But I figured what the hell, it was better than sitting around doing nothing. However, it's possible I sensed that an acting class might give me an opportunity to show people I was a cool, funny kid and not a geeky, awkward one. I had no reputation to overcome with these new kids.

The acting classes at Beginner's Showcase were taught by "well-known New York director" Jack Romano (make sure to r-r-roll that *R*), a gay, chain-smoking homunculus with copious opinions and an accent thick as a Cohiba cigar. Jack unwittingly became my first acting mentor.

I hesitated at the tent flap opening, then took a detour, ducking under a support rope. *I'll just wander around the tent for a minute and eavesdrop. Then I'll decide yay or nay.*

"Who the hell are you?" Jack Romano demanded when I finally slunk in.

"Uh, my name's Bill. I'm one of the film majors," I said, my heart clanging around my ribcage at his unexpected vehemence. "Bob said we should come join your class?"

"No, absolutely not. This is a class for *actors*. I don't care what Bob told you."

I must have looked sufficiently crestfallen for him to take pity on me.

"Oh, all right. Sit over there and stay out of the way."

Twenty or so teenage drama majors stared daggers at me while I scrounged a folding chair as far away from Jack as I could get.

"As I was saying, I want you all to sit still, close your eyes, and observe all the sounds you can hear around you," Jack instructed.

Pfft, I can do that. I'm a musician; I know how to listen.

I shut my eyes and concentrated. After a few minutes, people reported hearing the breeze blowing through trees, kids splashing in nearby Lake Sunapee, someone coughing. Pretty mundane stuff.

"Anybody hear anything else?" Jack asked.

I dared to lift my palm up to my chin. He scowled in my general direction.

"I heard my own breath and heartbeat, somebody licking their lips, Jack striking a match, and a song—I think it was 'In the Summertime'—playing on a car radio as someone drove by."

Jack's glare softened a bit. "What did you say your name was?"

"Bill."

"OK, Bill. Good job."

Maybe I'm in. I decided to keep coming back.

Tuition, room, and board at Beginner's Showcase cost $800 for eight weeks, the equivalent of about $5,000 in 2020 dollars. Campers toiled as cast and crew for productions both on the main stage (a converted barn) and in the tent theater. We produced musicals like *South Pacific*, *Man of La Mancha*, and *Brigadoon* in the barn. The tent was reserved for intimate dramas like *The House of Bernarda Alba*, *The Children's Hour*, and *The Empire Builders*. We worked our asses off putting up new shows every week. While we gained valuable experience, the camp directors undoubtedly profited from our "pay to play" labor. I'm not sure I'd call it exploitation but there was something not quite kosher going on.

Another thing that was apparently going on was sex—and plenty of it. Not for me, of course, given how unattractive and socially inept I felt. It seemed evident that at least some of the pretty boys and girls were hooking up. As an indication of the ubiquity of this behavior, some prankster climbed up on the roof of the barn to paint over the "P" on the huge sign that originally read "Beginner's Playhouse."

One afternoon, Phil and I barged in on a couple of counselors engaged in what I now know was mutual oral sex. All I saw then was limbs and heads; it looked like a giant writhing tarantula. As soon as the male counselor saw us, he waved frantically for us to get out of there. When I saw him in the barn later, he acted as if nothing untoward had occurred, which was fine by me. I was stung by what I'd seen and had zero desire to talk to anyone about it.

Another day that summer, Wayne and I wandered toward Lake Sunapee, intending to snag a canoe and row a few yards away from shore for some respite from the camp's chaos. As we neared the water, a shirtless middle-aged guy approached and leered unabashedly at each of us.

"You boys should be wearing athletic cups. I can see *everything* in your swim trunks."

Wayne and I exchanged a nervous glance and silently agreed to keep walking.

"Didn't you guys want a canoe or something?" the man called after us.

We couldn't get away from him fast enough. I didn't know the reason I needed to escape; the situation just felt incredibly threatening in the moment.

One evening, I was making my way up the ramp into the barn to report for my job as follow-spot operator for a performance of *Finian's Rainbow*. Bob, the camp director, was stationed at the entrance, jawing with a man standing shoulder to shoulder with him. As I was about to pass by, that squirrelly gray-haired man with a jack-o'-lantern grin grabbed ahold of my arm with one hand and, with the other, clawed each of my pubescent boy boobs, hard, in quick succession.

"You should be wearing a brassiere. Don't you think, Bob?"

The two men cackled. Time turned fish-eyed. I swiveled in slow motion from one hideous laughing face to the other. My mouth worked but I had no breath to form words. Time snapped back into place as I fled into the barn loft two steps at a time.

What the hell was that?

I fell, panting, onto a rickety bench, eyes glued to the top of the stairs, praying that creep hadn't followed me.

Weird men were taking a perverse interest in me. I felt powerless to defend myself, other than to run away. At the same time, my spigot of testosterone was wide open, stinking up my underarms, sprouting tufts of hair in random places on my face, and provoking intense lustful desires I didn't know how to manage. Men who repulsed me wanted something *from* me; girls I wanted to get close to seemed repulsed *by* me. I thought every camper besides me was having sex. *I'm a hopeless loser* was the only conclusion I could draw.

Eventually, I earned a modicum of respect from Jack. During one class, I played God as a smoking, philandering alcoholic during a humorous improvised scene, after which Jack commented, "Y'know, with some solid training you could be a successful comic actor."

After that, I was a momentary hit with my fellow students. The sexiest girl in class, who'd sat on my lap during the scene, spontaneously repeated that gesture for a minute after class. I was so nervous I couldn't enjoy it. If I'd been less petrified I might have parlayed that moment into something, but it turned into nothing but a few seconds of sweaty palms.

A couple of years later, in high school, I acquiesced to a request from my pal Nina Shengold to audition for a production of Noel Coward's *Blithe Spirit*, which she was directing. Nina's now a successful teacher, editor, and writer of plays, screenplays, young adult novels, and a great memoir. When, to my great surprise, Nina cast me in the supporting role of Dr. Bradman, I boomeranged between enthusiasm and dread. Was I really going to set foot on that huge stage, under those dazzling lights, in front of all those people?

Blithe Spirit was the first scripted play I'd ever done. The challenges were many: memorizing my lines and the blocking (how you're supposed to move onstage), speaking in a high British accent, and doing it loudly enough that my words carried to the far corners of our cavernous high school auditorium.

The cast and crew gave two performances over a weekend following a couple of months of after-school rehearsals. I thought things had gone well until I read the review in our local rag of a newspaper. The critic enjoyed the show but said something like this about my performance:

"Mr. Harrison seems to have missed the comic possibilities of his role as Dr. Bradman."

Me? Miss a comic opportunity? How humiliating. Jeez, why do they send theater critics to high school productions anyway? My first bad review, for my first performance as an actor. Check.

A year later, Nina nudged me into joining her student-run drama group where, in addition to other roles, I played the salacious theater critic Birdboot in Tom Stoppard's *The Real Inspector Hound*. During an early rehearsal of that show, I had to do a scene with Melanie, the actress playing the ingenue in Stoppard's play-within-a-play. We exchanged a line or two, then I was supposed to kiss her. This was going to be my first ever honest-to-goodness smack on the lips.

Melanie, bless her heart, sensed my trepidation and aggressively kissed me.

I'm not sure if and when I'd have ever gotten around to kissing anyone had it not been for that stage kiss.

Kissing wasn't the issue in Victor's class. The goal of Meisner's Repetition exercise is to help actors feel safe enough onstage to allow themselves to be seen—truly seen—with all of their flaws, foibles, and eccentricities on display.

The rules of the exercise are simple: Two actors face each other onstage. One of them makes an observation about the other, like "Great breasts!" The second actor must repeat exactly what the first one said until either person observes a change in the other's behavior that elicits a new statement, as in "You're embarrassed." Each actor strives to keep their attention on their partner and to stay in the moment.

When it works, there's a free flow of spontaneous interaction that's exciting and beautiful to behold. The work is so challenging because everyone has parts of themselves they would prefer to keep hidden. Progress occurs when actors learn to overcome their self-consciousness and permit their real emotional responses to be seen.

Victor would alternately cajole, wheedle, berate, and coddle us to get the results he wanted. As demanding as he was, he tempered his adamancy by reminding us that "this is a process." He acknowledged that it takes time to develop the ability to respond and behave truthfully. Vic sent me up there with the busty would-be actress that day because he thought I'd "be the only one in class brave enough to say it."

Classes were intimidating as hell. Victor encouraged courage and rejected fakery. He wanted his students to be as real, raw and forthcoming as possible. He stopped many an exercise by yelling "Too safe!" and sending the mortified pair of actors back to their seats. Victor told us that no one had ever died while doing the Repetition, though it often felt to me as if death was imminent (and might be preferable). For the first few weeks, I sat in the back row trying to will myself into invisibility so I wouldn't get called on to face the heat.

One semester Victor paired me with a particular actress week after week, because he intuited there was something significant happening between us that remained unexpressed. He kept pushing us to break through to whatever it was. Finally, after six weeks of torture (which I believe Vic enjoyed inflicting on us), the woman suddenly yelled:

"You disgust me! I hate you!"

"YES! I disgust you! You hate me!"

I clapped my hands and jumped up and down when she was finally able to speak her truth.

The first time I allowed myself to cry onstage, Victor said "Good, you opened that door. Now stick a brick in there and don't let it close on you."

Another metaphor he liked to use was water.

"You need to have all the faucets—fear, joy, sadness, anger, shame—open and flowing if you want to be an actor. If you don't like doing this, you should go to accounting school."

Yeah, subtle he was not.

Unsurprisingly, it was in the area of sexuality that Victor was most insistent. He was expert at sussing out the shades of attraction we so doggedly tried to avoid during our improvised scenes. His own exuberant homosexuality was, it seemed to me, an expression of pride as well as a model of openness he wanted us to emulate. Vic demanded full disclosure of the palette of emotions that got stirred up in conjunction with our sexual impulses. Despite my "brave" observation about that young woman's breasts, this was particularly daunting for me.

Most of my fellow students were half my age. The women were gorgeous, the men were handsome. And there I was, middle-aged, fat, a victim of creeping male-pattern baldness. Every damn class I had to confront the cesspool of emotions around this age and attractiveness chasm. And Victor was not about to allow me to avoid those feelings. He knew I needed to be able to access them in whatever work I might do as an actor. Nine times out of ten I'd feel drawn to whichever pretty young thing he sent me up there with. And ten times out of ten she'd rebuff me. I learned how to get out of my own way enough to express whatever those uncomfortable situations evoked in me—humiliation, frustration, anger, sadness.

I had problems of a different sort with some of the men I encountered for the Repetition. If any of them expressed even the tiniest hint of attraction to me, the trauma from the incident with the brassiere guy made me retreat to the farthest wall; I needed to get the hell away from whomever it was immediately.

No one asked why. As long as my behavior was clear, I was doing the exercise properly. But those scenes were troubling.

Vic and I had a memorable private conversation that activated memories of Beginner's Showcase a year or so into my training. He told me that he'd briefly experimented with heterosexuality in college and wondered if I'd done the same in reverse.

"C'mon," he insisted. "You must have sucked a cock or two at Northwestern."

I stood there, mouth agape like a dead guppy. "Uh, no, Vic. Not that I can remember."

He thought that was *hilarious*. I stared at the wall and tried not to let on that I found his delight appalling.

In the spring of 1998, Victor cast me in the role of Daddy in a production of Edward Albee's *The American Dream*. The week before he called to invite me to audition, I'd stumbled across and reread the dog-eared paperback copy of that play (paired in an ancient edition with *The Zoo Story*) I'd been schlepping around since high school. Coincidence or synchronicity?

The rehearsal process was an intense extension of the work we'd been doing in class. Victor employed some unusual methods, including pounding me on the chest to demonstrate how the behavior of one of the characters should "hit" me. Later in the process he whispered to me that he wanted Daddy to have a strong attraction to the other male character.

"Have it, and hide it," he directed.

The talented and dedicated cast of *The American Dream* performed four shows a week for a month and a half. I earned zero dollars during that period. And loved it.

Training with Victor in the Meisner technique went right to the heart of my lifelong internal conflict between fear and desire, between wanting to be invisible and longing to be seen, between self-imposed silence and the need to claim my selfhood loud and clear. Had he been alive to attend a performance of *The American Dream*, I like to think Jack Romano would have been p-r-r-roud.

The author having a fine time at Beginner's Showcase, c. 1972

Part IV

Turn of the Century

2001

"Say hello to Chita Rivera and John McMartin, everybody," David Loud, the conductor, tells our pit orchestra, gesturing toward center stage. The winds and brass sections applaud the two stars with their feet; the string players by tapping our bows on music stands. Ms. Rivera and Mr. McMartin gaze down at us and wave politely.

"Thanks to you all for bringing your artistry to the theater," Ms. Rivera says. "This is such a difficult time for everyone. Thank you so very much."

The cast, musicians, and crew have convened around the main stage at Goodman Theatre to begin rehearsals for the world premiere of *The Visit*. It's Monday, September 17, 2001.

Artistry? I dragged this empty shell of myself downtown without thought or sensation. I stand in the pit among my peers, a bag of bones clutching this wooden contraption so I don't fall down. I am surviving; if that's an art, then I'm finger painting.

Sometime during that first week of rehearsals, I received a call from a news producer at the local Fox News TV station. They wanted to tape an interview with me at the theater. Why me? No idea.

After clearing it with Goodman's PR department, a crew met me there a few hours before the next day's rehearsal. They recorded a few minutes of me doing some mournful *arco* improvising from the pit before we sat down for the interview.

"What's it like working in the theater so soon after the events of 9/11?" asked the neatly coiffed news guy.

"I mostly feel numb. My colleagues and I are making a valiant effort to stay focused on the play and the music. But—"

"It must be difficult to mount a show under these circumstances."

"Yeah, it is. It's both a dreadful time and a godsend to be together doing what we do. Rehearsing and performing is not only our job, but also our way of expressing ourselves. And right now it's a great distraction from . . . I guess I'd have to call it grief. I'm doing the best I can; we're all doing the best we can."

He asked me for a synopsis of *The Visit*, which I bungled my way through. What I wish I'd said was that the play tells the story of an older woman (Rivera) who returns to the small European village where she grew up to seek revenge against a man (McMartin) who had seduced then abandoned her when she was a teenager. The town is in the midst of a severe economic crisis, which, it turns out, the woman engineered. Now wealthy and powerful, she offers to infuse the local economy with cash, but in return they must agree to murder the man.

It was a chilling and beautiful piece of theatre. Emotions, onstage and off, were running high, due to both the play and real-world circumstances. I was especially moved by the distress of one ensemble member whose husband would be deployed to Iraq a few weeks into the show's run.

I will never forget the final heart-stopping tableau of *The Visit*, in which the townspeople are fanned out in an arc across the stage, staring silently with mouths agape at the audience, as they awaken to the hideousness of the crime they're about to commit. Goose bumps rose on my forearms at that moment every performance.

The Visit ran through the first week of November, after which the bottom dropped out of my calendar. Gigs were canceled right and left as individuals and businesses succumbed to the nation's collective trauma and fear. This sudden decline in employment after 9/11 rattled my cage. The hollowness in my chest was replaced by a knot of terror in my belly. For the first time since college, I had to seriously consider a more dependable occupation.

But what? I was pretty good at making the low notes but useless for most anything else I could think of. Going back to school to become, say, a schoolteacher or a librarian, seemed impossible. I wasn't going to work in a goddamn record store again. I had no savings to tap for tuition or other expenses. No, I needed something I could do *now*.

One February afternoon I was lounging on my couch, surveying the living room.

I can't manufacture more gigs; everyone I know is scuffling for jobbing and club work. There are no theater gigs on the horizon.

My eyes landed on the music stand I'd tucked into the corner by the window after the couple of bass lessons I'd taught that morning.

Teaching. Maybe I should try to rustle up more students. At $40 an hour, I could piece together a decent income if I had a dozen or so students per week. At the time, I had only three or four, depending on the week.

Yeah, but to get more bass pupils I'm going to have to do something I absolutely abhor: market myself. It's either that or move into my mother's attic—or starve. Oy vey. If those are the choices, I'll have to overcome my self-promotion allergy and find a way to advertise my teaching services.

In the words of Charlie Parker, now's the time.

Back to the Future

2003

Something had been brewing with my lower back for the previous ten days. I was working a low-budget, high-stress show with the unwieldy title *The Bubbly Black Girl Sheds Her Chameleon Skin* at the now long-gone Apple Tree Theatre in Highland Park. Between the soreness in my back and the ever-present ache in my left-hand index finger's knuckle, I wasn't having the best time. I always strove to play well, but I was especially motivated for this show. I enjoyed working with the music director and hoped doing a bang-up job for him might lead to more work. The music business was still recovering from 9/11 and I was feeling the squeeze of too little work.

One Friday night in the middle of the run, I drove home with more than the usual irritation in my lumbar region. While climbing the stairs carrying two bass guitars (one in my hand, one strapped to my back), I was attacked by an ice pick of pain in my sacroiliac. I fell flat on my face on the stairs as if I'd just been shot by a sniper. My next-door neighbor, a woman I hardly knew, must have heard my body *thunk*. She cracked open her door to investigate.

"Oh my God, what happened to you?" she cried. "Let me help you up."

"I don't think I can get up," I croaked. "But could you bring my stuff into my apartment?"

She disentangled the bass guitars as I fished the keys out of my pocket. She opened the door and placed the instruments in my hallway while I crawled the rest of the way upstairs and into my apartment. My neighbor pulled off my shoes and somehow helped me into bed.

"Thanks," I managed to say. "I owe you one."

"Don't worry about it. I hope you're better tomorrow."

How I made it through the night is a mystery. Early the next morning, still in paralyzing pain, I called my mother, who lived about a half hour west at the time. She had a bottle of hydrocodone squirreled away in her medicine chest, which she delivered post haste. The opioid took the edge off. I called my MD, who advised me to supplement the hydrocodone with 800 mg of ibuprofen every four hours.

Two decades had passed since I'd last battled serious physical challenges. I had fully recovered from the appendectomy but was not so fortunate with the broken finger. The soreness in the knuckle was chronic and unpredictable. It bugged the hell out of me whenever it flared up. That finger ache vanished as the meds for my back took effect. I'd forgotten what living without relentless pain felt like.

The potent combination of painkillers brought me to the cusp of sleep. Before drifting off into what would be sixteen hours of uninterrupted snoozing, I managed to call the music director. "Tom. Hey, it's Bill."

"Hi. What's up."

"I'm sorry to say that I won't be able to play the show tonight."

"Wait, why not? What happened?"

"I wrenched my back somehow when I got home last night, and basically, I can't move right now."

"Oh, man. Sorry to hear that. Well, rest up. I'll do what I can to cover your parts with my left hand. I'll look forward to seeing you Sunday. Keep me posted, will you?"

"Of course, yeah. Thanks."

I had serious doubts that I'd ever get out of bed again, let alone play the bass, but I managed to keep those catastrophic imaginings to myself. My final thought before I drifted off was *I'm barely hanging on as it is. Now this? What the fuck.*

Sunday morning, my full-to-the-gills bladder woke me up. I squirmed around a bit on the bed, anticipating a surge of pain. Nothing. I rolled over from my back to my side. Still nada. I swung my legs over the edge of the bed and wobbled to a standing position—pain free. It was a freakin' miracle.

As I ambled around the apartment in slow motion, I expected to be struck down with sudden agony any second. No, I was really OK.

I poured a bowl of Cheerios and called the music director to tell him I'd see him in a few hours for the Sunday matinee.

Back from the precipice of disaster once again. When was my luck with recovering from these potential calamities going to run out?

When I received my check the following week, I'd been docked for the show I missed. Welcome to show biz, where there's no such thing as a sick day.

Necessity Is a Mother

2004–2006

These first several years of the new century weren't boding well. It was as if I'd been transported back to the late 1970s, when every month was an adventure in subsistence. I had succeeded in expanding my teaching load. The freelance music business was painstakingly clawing its way out of the depths of post-9/11 despair. Still, there wasn't enough dough coming in to keep up with the exorbitant mortgage on the house I had purchased in '04 or to cover my health insurance. Food? Gas? Good luck, pal.

My physical health worried me. The soreness in both my lower back and my index finger were an unwelcome constant. Some days were worse than others, but the discomfort was omnipresent. The one activity that reliably caused the misery to spike was playing the bass.

Creative projects, the fuel for my musical engine, had all but withered away. Music, for the most part, had become the thing I did to make money. And, at this point in time, unless you had a steady touring gig or were a member of a full-time symphony orchestra, attempting to make a living playing music was a piss-poor choice. Without the juice from playing engaging material with great musicians, much of the fulfillment I used to get from music went dormant.

As had been the case twenty-five years earlier for a different cocktail of reasons, something had to be done. I didn't know what. This time, though, I didn't have Mr. Bruno, Mrs. Devirgilio, Ruth, Lindy, or my parents to see me through.

It was time to get creative. On my own.

"One . . . two . . . one, two, three, four," intones the Indiana-inflected voice of Jamey Aebersold, purveyor of jazz play-along tracks on LPs, cassettes, and CDs. He counts off the tempo on every track with the same flat Midwestern monotone. It's either humorous or annoying, depending on my mood. Lately it's been driving me bonkers.

Play-along (or backing) tracks are recordings of songs or chord progressions with one instrument missing from the mix. For instance, backing tracks for bass players might have piano or guitar and drums; the "live" bassist plays along with the other instruments as if they were sitting in with a band.

I'd been using Aebersold's backing tracks with my students because they were the only tracks on the market. Since the bass is primarily an accompaniment instrument, bassists need to practice with a rhythm section regularly. Most students, however, don't have a pianist and drummer in their back pocket. Play-along tracks are the next best thing.

Teaching had become my one constant source of income, which is not what I had in mind when I chose to go into music as a profession. I could live with that for the time being. However, between the financial woes, the paucity of creative opportunities, and the physical ailments, I wondered daily about the wisdom of my career choices.

A debate took place in my mind after a particularly unpleasant lesson I taught one day:

What if I were to create my own play-along tracks? Tracks I'd enjoy using and sharing with others.

You should go for it.

Nah, there's no way. I know zilch about creating a business like that from scratch.

OK, hold on a sec. You put together a teaching website last year, right? You learned some HTML, you worked with a graphic designer, you wrote all the website text, didn't you?

Yeah, but this is a whole other thing. I'd need an MBA for a project like this.

And...?

Shit, this is crazy talk, man.

Is it, though? You've done tough stuff before.

Sure, but—

Quit sputtering and think it through. It's a damn good idea.

You really think so?

Yeah I do.

Well, huh. If I do it I'm going to need a lot of help.

I dragged my feet for a few more months before I got fed up enough to call my audio engineer friend Jim.

"Are you going to make backing tracks exclusively for bass players?" Jim asks.

"No, I think . . . as long as I'm going to do this, why not create tracks anyone can use?"

"Like, piano, bass, and drums trios for horn players? And different configurations for each rhythm section player?"

"Yeah, something like that."

"You gotta do 'em in all twelve keys."

"Man, great idea. Joe Daley would be proud."

"So how are you going to get the products into your customers' hands?"

"Ooh, right. I'm not sure but I'm thinking I'll post them on a website and sell them via digital download. I don't want to have to press CDs and do mail order."

"Uh huh. CDs would get expensive, plus eat up a lot of time. Anyway, the whole concept sounds cool. Count me in."

Next I contacted Jeff Lane, the exceptional graphic designer who'd built my teaching website. We discussed the potential structure for this new venture that I was tentatively calling PlayJazzNow. The new site was going to be complex, which meant there'd be a substantial upfront investment to get the thing rolling. I was going to have to refinance my house to get my paws on some cash in order to make it happen. Risky business, for sure, but after mulling my conversations with Jim and Jeff, I decided to go all in.

Jeff got cracking on the website. I started researching the business side of things—a mysterious domain about which I knew nothing. I read books with titles like *Small Business for Dummies*. I conferred with Helena Bouchez, my friend from the marketing universe, to get her advice on the look and feel of the website as well as on how to make the site visible on a shoestring budget.

Sticky fundamental questions arose: How would I process payments? How was I going to distribute the tracks once customers bought them? I really was going to need a DIY MBA to go through with this zany plan.

I sought the assistance of others for their advice, sure. Mostly, though, I needed some validation from people I trusted to tell me the truth. Was this business really a good idea or was I kidding myself? Have I overlooked some major flaws which would ultimately lead to disaster?

At long last, I turned my attention to the musical content, the one area I felt confident about. I chose the initial batch of backing tracks, wrote arrangements, hired musicians, and booked recording time with Jim. Once we got into the studio I'd be the producer, the guy who organizes the sessions and pays for everything. I'd decide which takes were keepers and which ones needed a do-over. I was going to play bass on everything as well. After three decades as a sideman, this leadership role was a welcome, if disquieting, change.

One of my initial worries was that the musicians I hired for the sessions would think the idea for the website was stupid; that they would do the sessions solely for the money. If the business didn't pass muster with my peers, what would that say about it—and me? Tectonic murmurings of shame rumbled inside me with every phone call to a colleague.

"Hey, Karl," I said to my pianist friend's voice mail. "Bill Harrison here. Hey, man, I'm recording some play-along tracks for my new business and wondering if you'd be up for playing a couple of sessions next Wednesday and Thursday? Gimme a buzz when you can."

"Bill, how's it going?" Karl responded a few hours later. "That sounds cool, yeah. Count me in."

Which was the essence of what I heard from most of the musicians I contacted. Turns out they were glad to be involved with a project that had the potential to help beginning and intermediate jazz players. We all remembered how tricky it was to find high-quality practice materials when we were coming up. Once I understood that everyone was onboard, I was able to relax and concentrate on creating the music.

Over the next several years, I released hundreds of backing tracks, wrote a brief curriculum for beginning improvisers, created desktop and mobile apps, and used my teaching, acting, and filmmaking skills to produce more than fifty teaching videos. You can find them on YouTube.

As with so many other endeavors, I approached PlayJazzNow with a mutable blend of audacity and timidity. One minute I was proudly sending out emails trumpeting the release of new tracks; the next I was ensuring that my name was mentioned only on one obscure page of the website. I used the pseudonym "Trackmeister," which was the way I identified myself in PJN's marketing materials and in communications with customers.

PlayJazzNow never became profitable as a business. After three years of buckets of red ink, the site moved slightly into the black by 2010. However, I believe it's served a valuable purpose as a teaching tool. The tracks have been downloaded tens of thousands of times by students, teachers, and players of all stripes.

I can't claim that PlayJazzNow was absolutely the first site to offer downloadable jazz play-along tracks, but I can confirm that any number of copycat sites sprang up on the web by 2010. Even Jamey eventually started selling his tracks as digital downloads.

I used the ticks of a metronome in lieu of my voice to count off the play-along tracks on PJN. Some customers expressed particular appreciation for the clicks instead of Aebersold's flat-as-an-LP vocal count-offs.

Man, I just followed the hip-o-cratic oath: First, don't be annoying.

For All We Know

1979–2006

> Whatever is unnamed ... whatever is omitted ... whatever is mis-
> named as something else—this will become not merely unspoken,
> but unspeakable.
>
> —Adrienne Rich
> *On Lies, Secrets, and Silence 1966–1978*

"**A**nd here's my bass player, Bill Harrison. He looks like one of the seven dwarfs with that beard, don't you think? Sleepy or Doc." Al "Mr. Flying Fingers" Morgan's attempt at humor fell flat on its condescending face. I stage-whispered, "More like Dopey" from my post behind my bass, then heard a loud female guffaw from near the front of the house.

That's how I met a woman I'll call Emma in early 1979. She was in the audience for Al's show at Field's Supper Club in south sub-urban Oak Lawn, Illinois, because Al's drummer was her boyfriend. Al Morgan was in his seventh decade of banging on the piano and croaking out his hit "Jealous Heart." The band referred to him as "Mr. Flying Electrocardiogram." Emma, a beauty in her mid-twenties, was easy to spot in his audience, for whom the average age was Medicare.

Emma was one of the most luscious women I'd ever met—five foot two, eyes of brown, a swirl of chestnut hair, and an impish smile. She was a jazz singer, a fact which later in my life would have sent me screaming into the night. At the time, however, I thought, *Good God, what else is perfect about you?*

I fell for Emma like no one else before or since. She possessed an energetic optimism and an irresistibly wicked sense of humor. That she was a singer who knew so much of the same music I knew and loved made her all that more attractive. *Thud* went my heart, soul, and genitals.

The disappearance of her boyfriend a few weeks after we met opened the door of hope that she and I could be a "thing." I lived with this fervent desire for years, but Emma just wasn't into me like that. I had to settle for the close, platonic friendship we developed in the first few months of getting to know one another.

Emma and I played voice and bass duets in my living room. We did some trio gigs with my guitarist friend Dave. We went out for meals and had long heart-to-heart conversations late into many nights. We were the kind of friends who would have bailed one another out any time of day or night.

There was just one fatal flaw in our relationship: as much as I loved her, I couldn't find a way to honestly like Emma's singing. I tried to close my ears to her errant sense of pitch, her sometimes questionable taste, and her forays into scat singing (which I don't much like even when it's done well). How could I ever express anything close to my true opinion about her musical abilities without hurting her terribly and undoubtedly ruining our friendship? I was paralyzed by this internal dissonance.

So I did what any reasonable person would do—kept the truth to myself.

I visited Emma when she moved to the Pacific Northwest and, years later, when she relocated to Southern California. We continued to perform together sporadically, despite my misgivings. I never was able to quell my desire for her, despite the constantly shifting circumstances of both our lives.

In 2004, when I was first contemplating PlayJazzNow, I called Emma to see what she thought of the idea. She'd been earning a living coaching private vocal students and would surely have some good ideas about what kind of play-along tracks jazz vocal students might find useful.

"Hey, so I was thinking," Emma began during one of our phone chats. "Why don't we collaborate on some vocal tracks?"

"What do you mean?" I asked.

"Let's pick, like, half a dozen tunes. You write the arrangements and I'll come into town to record the demo tracks. We'll split the costs and each use the tracks for both our businesses."

"Well—"

"C'mon. It'll be fun. We haven't played together in years."

"Huh. It sure would be nice to see you. Lemme think about it."

Emma was right that it would be great to reconnect as friends, as it had been a long while since we'd seen one another. I knew she'd picked up considerable business savvy in the interim, which was something I lacked.

On the other hand, I was hesitant to commit to using her voice on my tracks. I feared there'd be musical problems that would be difficult to address without disclosing some of my honest feelings about her vocal limitations. I'd essentially been hiding my opinion of something so fundamental to our relationship for all of these years. What remained unspoken had become unspeakable.

Maybe things have changed, I thought. Maybe she's gotten a lot better since I last heard her sing. Maybe this project could be an opportunity for us to do something creative and potentially lucrative together. This line of thinking was so tantalizing that I ultimately couldn't resist saying yes to Emma's proposal. At the same time, there was this nagging voice inside my head whispering: *This is a very bad idea, and you're going to be sorry you agreed to it.*

That small voice was right. Things fell apart in a hurry in the studio. After a couple of takes of "But Not For Me," neither of which were usable, I could feel the other musicians' patience start to wane. I caught Jim's eye behind the studio glass for a flash of confirmation that I was hearing what I was hearing. It was not good.

We muddled through the other five tunes I'd agreed to record with Emma. The session ended with her and her current beau bubbly with excitement and me trying to put on a happy face through my disappointment. After everyone else left, Jim and I listened back to a couple of the tracks in the control room.

"Yeah, man. I don't know about this," Jim said.

"I know. What the hell am I gonna do?"

"You could hire another singer to record these tracks."

"Nah, I can't do that, Jim. She's my friend from way back. I let her talk me into it, and now I'm stuck. Crap."

How was I going to break the news to Emma? We were going to have to have the conversation I'd been avoiding for more than twenty years.

"I don't know how to say this any other way, my friend, but I don't think I can use these tracks on the website," I mumbled into the phone.

"What? What do you mean?" Emma said, her voice rising.

"Uh..."

"There's something wrong with them?"

"Um, they're not as good as I was anticipating."

"And you think that's because of me?"

I was silent, backed into a corner, and she knew it.

"You're not saying anything. You think I fucked up the recordings? Do you?"

"I wouldn't put it that way—"

Emma, temper barely under control, went on to explain that she planned to "fix up" the vocal tracks once she had the master recordings in her possession. She claimed that what she recorded during our session were "scratch tracks"—temporary, like placeholder performances, sung only to give the band something to react to during the takes. This was bullshit. We never talked about doing scratch tracks; these were supposed to be final performances, ready to be mixed and released. Now it was my turn to burn.

"I'm sorry, Emma. You know very well we never discussed scratch tracks. Were you planning to go into a studio and rerecord all your vocal tracks? Come on."

"I was planning on fixing things up, yeah. I had a sinus infection that day."

That was the first I heard of this health issue as well. Emma and I had a few conversations in this vein before we gave up trying to dig our way out of this pit of mutual frustration. Emma suggested we engage the services of a mediator to negotiate the fate of the tracks. I readily agreed.

The only communication we had after that was via the mediator. Once we reached an agreement it was clear that our relationship was kaput. We haven't been in touch since, which has been a terrible loss for me. It was only after this final cutoff that I realized I was going to have to mourn both the loss of the friendship and the permanent shutting down of the romantic fantasies I still harbored for her.

I wish I'd done things differently, but I don't feel entirely responsible for the demise of our friendship. I'd hidden a fundamental truth from my friend, but she wasn't straightforward with me either in the aftermath of the fateful recording session.

The final song Emma sang with us in the studio that day was "For All We Know," with its poignant lyrics that copyright law prevents me from quoting.

Music by the Pound[1]

2005–2017

> As soon as we unpack our instruments we're too loud.
> —Anonymous jobbing musician from days of yore

"**D**o you think anyone would notice if we mime playing but don't actually make any sound?" I ask my drummer friend Nick Coconato at some corporate "background music" gig.

"Yeah, probably not," he says with a smirk. "We should try it and see."

"How long before somebody comes running up to tell us we're too loud?" adds Peter.

"Any minute now," says Jim M., picking up his tenor sax.

As if on cue, a harried flunky sidles up to the bandstand and stage whispers, "Hey, guys, it's a bit too loud. Can you tone it down?"

We can hardly contain our dark, knowing laughter.

Sliced. Diced. Mashed. Poached. Seared. Raw. Burned to a cinder. Scoop a handful of musicians into a pot and simmer us on a back burner. We'll serve up as many pounds of innocuous notes as you need for your cocktail party, dinner, convention, sales meeting, awards banquet—whatever.

Ah, the background music gig, where musicians are hired as animated wallpaper, providing sophisticated aural ambience designed to be ignored by everyone present. These kinds of jobs are like Heinz 57; there are many varieties but they're all pickles.

Here's how it works: Businesses engage the services of consultants, known as event planners, who book a venue, hire caterers, rent

---

1   I cannot take credit for this phrase. It was coined by my witty friend Marc Perlish.

A/V equipment, and contract entertainment. Sometimes a business, also known as "the end-client," wants a comedian, a motivational speaker, a DJ, or a dance band. More often than not, however, especially since the turn of the century, these clients want a small ensemble to stay out of the way while their employees, customers, or boards of directors eat, drink, schmooze, and pat themselves on the back.

The end-client *thinks* they want music. They *say* they want music. What they really want is people who *look* like musicians but who don't make too much noise. The event planner who hires us, usually an officious overdressed go-getter in their twenties, gives the bandleader precise orders about the type of music the end-client allegedly wants. This micro-management is as vexing as it is moot. The corporate client's number one priority is that the event runs without any hiccups. And what they most want from musicians is for us to be inconspicuous.

"When does the mike pounding start?" Peter wonders aloud.

That's the inevitable moment when some suit walks up to the podium and, as if we're invisible, starts tapping on the microphone. We have to jam on the brakes immediately.

"You know it's coming," I say to my friend.

Thump, thump, thump. "Hello? Can I have your attention please?"—obligatory feedback—"The silent auction will be closing in fifteen minutes. Also, the bar is open!"

Earlier in my career I relished these background gigs. They were a welcome respite from meat-and-potatoes jobbing, the pain-in-the-ass private parties that transform musicians into human jukeboxes loaded with 45s none of us want to play. The songs themselves morph over time, but the lowest common denominator vibe doesn't.

A representative musical autopsy from the '70s to '90s jobbing repertoire includes the venerable "Hokey Pokey," "The Chicken Dance," "The Electric Slide," "Celebration," "Achy Breaky Heart," "Margaritaville," and "Sweet Caroline." And let's not forget the lovely ballads: "Wind beneath My Wings," "That's What Friends Are For," and "Saving All My Love for You," a song about infidelity that was inexplicably played for innumerable first dances at weddings. Typing this list makes me want to go take a shower.

There were many times, while whanging out a stirring rendition of, say, "Louie Louie," that I thought, *So this is why I learned to play Coltrane's "Giant Steps" at 200 BPM, huh?*

Background music gigs, what musicians sometimes refer to as "jazz jobbing," were, as I say, a nice contrast. No overbearing mother of the bride, obnoxious uncle, toasted best man, tossing of the bouquet, or the removal of the bride's garter (during which we were required by law to play "The Stripper"). Just tell us what corner to set up in and leave us to stew in our own *au jus*.

We'd play for one another. As long as we kept the volume in check, we could play pretty much anything. Every once in a great while, someone from the crowd would come up to us on a break and say, "I know it seems like no one's listening, but I am. And you guys sound great."

That was then. By the mid-2000s, however, these "music by the pound" jobs magnified the frustrations that had been creeping into my consciousness for at least the past decade. As performers, we have a strong instinct to want to connect with our audience. We want to matter, to be an integral part of the meal being served. We don't have to be the entrée; it's OK if we're relegated to *amuse bouche* status.

This is the primary reason I preferred working in the theater. Playing Broadway-type shows is the polar opposite of these somnambulistic gigs, because what musicians do in the pit absolutely matters. Even if your individual contributions to the overall production go unnoticed by the audience, it's unquestionably true that each of us—actors, musicians, crew—are mutually dependent. The show can veer off course in a flash if any one of us commits an egregious enough error. Our tacit commitment to one another is the essential ingredient for staying focused on the complex recipe that makes or ruins a show.

As refreshing as it was to skip the father/daughter dance and the hora medley, there was little solace in knowing that Jim, Peter, Nick, and I could either pretend to play or actually suck and easily get away with it on most of these background music jobs. Little did I know that the most ridiculous version of "faking it" was right around the corner.

Jazz jobbing with the Amelot bass, c. 2010

I'm Not a Real Bass Player,
I Just Play One on TV

2011

"Oooh, I've always wanted to put this in a show," this episode's director tells me. "When we get to that spot in the song, you grab Laura around the waist and spin both her and your bass toward the front of the stage."

Oh no. This is the stupidest—

"That sounds great!" Laura, the star of the show, chimes in.

Mm-kay. So—I'm going to wrap my chunky arm around this magnificent woman, who's clad only in a skimpy black bunny outfit and stilettos, and twirl her and the bass?

"Take one. Rolling."

The cue comes. I reach around Laura and, in my nervousness, grasp her about twelve inches too high—right under her bustier.

"Cut! Let's do one more."

My face flares crimson. Laura, good sport that she is, gives me a knowing wink.

"Hey, maybe not quite so . . . tight this time, OK?" she says.

"Sure," I squeak.

We do better on takes two, three, and four but the shot winds up on the cutting room floor. It would have been my network TV "dancing" debut.

A few weeks earlier I'd met up with Nick to audition for this new TV series, *The Playboy Club*, which was about to start shooting in Chicago. We showed up more or less on a lark. I almost didn't bother. I figured the chances of my getting chosen from the pool of bass players based solely on my looks was slim to none. On the way out, Nick caught up with me.

"Wouldn't it be cool if we both snagged this gig?" he posited.

"Sure, that'd be fun. I doubt it's gonna happen, but yeah."

And then it did. The producers didn't hire us to *play* music. They hired us to *mime* playing to prerecorded tracks. *Whatever*, I thought. A gig is a gig is a gig. *This will be just like all those background music gigs we've played, except we'll be on the tube instead of stuffed into the corner of some ballroom.*

The timing was auspicious, given how the music industry had gotten pummeled by the '07–'08 financial crisis. The dough from this job would help bail me out a little. And my kids would get a laugh out of my pretending to be a bass player on TV.

Both Nick and I had worked at the real Playboy Club, though not together. Chicago was home to the original club, which opened in 1960. For several years, it was the busiest and most profitable bar/restaurant in town. By the mid-80s, though, the faux-1950s vibe had lost most of its luster. Playboy Clubs in other cities fared better, but Chicago's club closed its doors in 1986.

I played there a couple of times in my late twenties with a jazz trio. My internal radiator was cranked pretty high at the thought of seeing some barely clad, fluffy-tailed servers hopping around the premises in the flesh. But the bandstand was situated in an isolated corner of the club, where we were surrounded by a claustrophobic crush of leering middle-aged men swarming in a noxious cloud of cigar smoke. I never spied any bunnies through the haze. The gagging and burning in my eyes was the antithesis of sexy. But a gig is a gig is a gig.

My own connection to *Playboy*, if one can call it that, dates back to preadolescence. The magazine debuted in 1953, a propitious cultural moment for members of my parents' generation, who came of age during the leading edge of the so-called sexual revolution. My father was certainly an avid, uh, reader.

Around 1966, when I was nine, the following *sotto voce* conversation took place between my parents during an episode of the *Batman* TV show that featured the alluring Julie Newmar as Catwoman:

"I've seen *all* of her," quipped my father.

"She's been in *Playboy*?" my mother asked in a bored monotone.

"Oh, yeah. Several times."

Wait, was he drooling?

I was thunderstruck. People talked about this kind of stuff *out loud?* I scrunched down on the sofa, trying to make myself as small as possible, hoping my parents wouldn't notice me sitting there tuned in to this exchange.

My own introduction to the world of glossy two-dimensional naked women, like that of millions of other pubescent boys, came via *Playboy* magazine. For me, it happened at Harrison All Discount Center, my father's retail electronics store at 103rd Street and Broadway in Manhattan. He would occasionally invite me to go to work with him on Saturdays. I always jumped at the chance, because what boy doesn't want to spend time alone with his dad? My jobs there were sweeping the floor and stacking boxes of radios, TVs, and stereos down in the dungeon of a basement. Grunt work for sure, but I felt like *somebody* there.

I laid eyes on naked women—or rather, pictures of them—for the first time in the grody basement bathroom of Dad's store. The walls were covered with an eye-popping collage of *Playboy* centerfolds. When he gave me the initial tour of the place, my father admonished me to "leave my girls alone." For a while I obeyed that dictum, but once I realized no one would notice or care, I'd surreptitiously tear a page or two from the magazines stacked up on the floor—for research purposes only, of course.

It's hard to convey just how arousing those photos were to my prepubescent self. "Pulse-pounding" is a cliché, but that phrase precisely describes how my body reacted to those images. In retrospect, the pictures were charmingly innocent compared to the variety of raunch available these days at the tap of a screen. But to young straight men of my generation, Playboy was the *sine qua non* of salacious entertainment. It certainly got my juices flowing.

Despite the evolving zeitgeist of the '60s and '70s, sexuality was a taboo topic in my family. I wasn't given the "birds and the bees" talk. My father's contribution to my sex education was to tease me when he thought I had a crush on a classmate. My mother was equally mum on the subject, even after she discovered a purloined photo of a busty Playmate I'd carelessly left in my chinos pocket on laundry day. She fished it out and left it, folded origami-like, on my desk. I flushed with shame when I saw that she'd found incontrovertible evidence of my evil perversity. That was the last time I brought one of those pictures home.

The producers of *The Playboy Club* somehow convinced NBC that a crime drama set in Chicago's Playboy Club in 1961 would make for good television in 2011. It seemed like a dubious proposition to me, but I just make the low notes. Or, in this case, pretend to.

Thus, one gloomy March 2011 morning, I drove to Cinespace, a soundstage on the West Side, and presented myself to one of the assistant directors. She showed me to the men's costume area, where I met the other band members. I was pleasantly surprised to see that the producers had chosen to split the band racially; there were three Black and three white men, something that's unlikely to have occurred in real life in 1961. And what better way is there to meet your colleagues than when you're all in your skivvies? There were no female musicians, of course, because this was, after all, *The Playboy Club*. The women in the show had to be dressed in bunny outfits or less.

I donned a tuxedo and a pair of the most uncomfortable shoes I've ever worn, then reported to the makeup department. This routine was sort of fun the first time or two but it got old real quick, especially those lethal shoes.

The only thing the guys in the band knew regarding that first day was that we'd be filming a scene in which the head bunny (if that's the appropriate sobriquet), played by the wicked and wonderful Laura Benanti, would be singing the old standard "Chicago." We'd be miming along with a truly terrible prerecorded arrangement.

So it's come to this.

But a gig is a gig is a gig.

Filming a TV show involves a *lot* of waiting, something I'd learned on my own *Star Trek* set decades earlier. Our band cooled its heels interminably. All that sitting around gave me plenty of time to ponder the evolution of my relationship to *Playboy* and, by association, my sexuality. I was no longer the acne-ridden, hormone-drenched prepubescent who was convinced I had to bury my attraction to Jody and other girls. The dreadful shame I tortured myself with then was long gone; and good riddance. Yet here I was, in my mid-fifties, still getting a flash of lustful arousal—a catch in my lungs, an acceleration of my heartbeat—entering a TV version of a Playboy club. The stark difference between then and now: I felt no need to hide my reactions, to pretend I was cool when I wasn't. I had to smile at this realization. It was about damn time I got comfortable being human.

As soon as the director needed us, the six of us had to literally run to the set and assume our positions on the stage. We worked for maybe seventy-five minutes out of the fourteen hours we spent at Cinespace. While filming the "Chicago" scene, a few of us grew antsy between takes. We reflexively bleeped and blooped a note or two while Laura was trying to work out some dance steps to go along with lip-synching to the track she'd recorded.

"Hey, guys, would you cool it? I'm trying to figure this out."

Duly chastened, we made some apologetic noises, to which the actress responded, "Sorry. I can be a little cunty sometimes."

That broke the tension. After Laura asked us the proper way to pronounce "motherfucker" Chicago style, she transformed in my eyes from a glamorous, untouchable Playboy bunny into a regular person. When she and I later did that embarrassing "dance" take, I might have spontaneously combusted had we not already shared this moment of "we're all just doing our jobs."

The Playboy Club premiered on September 19. The final episode aired on October 3. The show became the first casualty of the 2011–12 television season after only the first three episodes were broadcast. Its ratings were dismal. Members of the prudish Parents Television Council and a smattering of other antipornography groups (none of whom, I'm quite certain, watched a single episode) called for boycotts of the show, which didn't help. Other critics bemoaned the paucity of sexual content, which they claimed made the show too tame. *The Playboy Club* pleased no one all of the time, probably because of the risqué reputation of Playboy as an institution.

Ultimately, the producers filmed seven episodes, hoping to sell the show to a different network. I worked on four of them. We heard rumors of a deal with cable network Bravo; later there was scuttlebutt about the show getting released on DVD. None of that transpired, which was a drag.

Alas, the show's cancelation dashed my fantasy of a spin-off, tentatively titled *Playboy Club: All about That Bass (Player)*. Hey, a guy can dream.

The author with Laura Benanti on the set of *The Playboy Club*, 2011

No Rest for the Wicked

2007; 2010–2011

My cell phone buzzed. It was Tim Burke, the contractor and lead trumpet player for the production of *Wicked* that ran from 2005 through 2009 at Chicago's Oriental Theater.

"Hey, Tim. What's up?"

"Hi, Bill. Are you going to be back at the theater soon?"

I looked at my phone. 7:20 p.m. *Dude, why are you calling me? The curtain is 8 p.m. I'm less than a block away.*

"Yeah, sure. I'll be there in time."

"OK, see you soon."

I was subbing for Tom Mendel, the show's regular bassist, on a two-show Wednesday. I'd played the matinee and was enjoying my dinner break. I went back to my tea and book. My phone lit up again at 7:28. *What the hell?*

"Hey, Bill," Tim said with alarm. "It's a seven thirty downbeat. Where are you?"

"Holy shit!"

I slammed my book shut and ran down the alley toward the stage door. The first notes of the overture came roaring up the stairs like a tsunami as soon as I got buzzed into the backstage area. I ran like hell, my heart in my esophagus, and made it to the pit less than a minute into the first number. I was shaking so much I could barely pick up my bass. I'm sure my face was ashen. I couldn't look anyone in the eye. *That's it. This is my last gig ever. No one will ever hire me again.*

The first act ended. I sat down heavily on the stool in the bass booth, waiting for the boom to be lowered. The contractor and the music director converged and asked me what had happened. I told them the truth.

"I'm so sorry. I had it in my head that the downbeat was eight, not seven thirty."

"I thought maybe that was the case. That's why I called you," said Tim.

"Sorry for being so dense."

"Well, good thing Rick [the first keyboardist] covered your parts while you were AWOL," interjected Colin, the music director. "I don't think anyone of consequence noticed your absence but you absolutely cannot let this happen again."

I hung my head. The two of them wandered off, though not before I spied the flicker of a secret smile from Tim, who I imagine might have made a similar blunder sometime in his long career.

Goddamn, I was so sure I was right.

I'd been offended that Tim called, when all he'd been trying to do was save my ass. That streak of arrogance was still alive in me. And it had almost cost me my reputation.

In December of 2010, the national tour of *Wicked* flew into Chicago for an eight-week run. Tim called me not to sub but to play the whole run, which was very cool of him. This time the challenges were physical and mental, not chronological.

Wicked is a taxing show. The orchestrator keeps bass players on their toes for the entire two-hour-and-forty-five-minute run time. You're leaping back and forth between upright, five-string electric, and fretless bass, sometimes with mere seconds to make the switch. Each instrument requires a lightning-fast technical recalibration to account for differences in string length, frets/no frets, right-hand touch, and relative volume. There's little downtime. It takes energy and focus. It's what you're getting paid the big bucks to do.

"Popular," one of the most popular numbers in the show, is a good example. The first section of the song is played on upright bass. It's a tricky few bars that's rather exposed (i.e., there's no place to hide in the sonic weeds). Then you've got to basically throw down the big dog and grab the fretless bass—as silently as you can. When the song goes into tempo, you've got to be right on the money with both pitch and rhythm because, once again, the orchestration is sparse. If

I wasn't already sweating this would be the moment that would do it, show after show.

Though this run was only two or three years after the many times I'd subbed on the Chicago production of *Wicked*, my body had a tough time adjusting to the intensity of these eight-show weeks. My lower back ached all the time, playing bass or not. My entire left hand—not just the injured forefinger—was on fire every night by the time Act II began. I tried ibuprofen, icing, heating, and slathering Voltaren arthritis gel, which stank up the pit and didn't help much.

Flashbacks of slogging through the first weeks of *Bye Bye Birdie* intruded during performances. I was finding it difficult to concentrate.

What was happening to me? Was my body betraying me now that I was in my fifties? Was I going to have to quit doing shows?

Wicked could be a fun show to play, but not when you're in this kind of anguish.

A few months after this run, a demonic force grabbed my lumbar region with its steely talons and clamped down. It took all the effort I could muster to crawl to the plush cocoa-colored couch in my living room and flop there. I was unable to move. Any attempt to adjust any part of my body sent immediate shockwaves of agony through me.

Why, why, why? What wicked thing did I do to bring on this torment?

Last time the reasons for the back attack were clearly work related. *Wicked* and *The Playboy Club* were months ago. I was hardly working now. Where did *this* come from?

I wasn't nearly as lucky with meds as I'd been the previous time. No one I knew had any adult painkillers and my current doctor refused to prescribe anything serious unless I went to his office. I explained the situation, that I was unable to sit or stand up, but he was adamant. I considered calling 911 for a ride to the ER, but because I couldn't afford health insurance, I was terrified of the potential financial fallout.

So I laid there for five days, ingesting gobs of ibuprofen—a popgun for a charging rhinoceros—with juice or water, because getting to the bathroom to empty my bowels was out of the question. My partner, Nina, wanted to help but her psychotherapy practice kept her downtown all day most days. One afternoon, my twenty-three-year-old son came by to visit and kindly brought me a tuna salad sandwich.

I spent endless hours lying in the dark, playing *Angry Birds* on my iPhone, waiting for some relief to fall from the sky.

Eventually, whatever satanic spirit had possessed the lower third of my back loosened its diabolical grip enough so that I was able to walk to Nina's car. She drove us to her Printer's Row loft, where I convalesced for another week before I could tentatively resume vertical life.

"I'm really at a loss," I confessed to Nina.

"It was hard seeing you in that kind of pain," she said.

"Yeah. I mean, I'm fifty-five. I've got no retirement savings. My back is clearly messed up. My stupid finger hurts all the damn time. What the hell am I supposed to do?"

"Well, you've been through a lot of crap lately. I know because you've been even crabbier than usual."

"Real nice . . ."

"Just teasing. You know I've got your back."

"Yeah, I know. And good pun."

I'd always assumed I'd play music until I keeled over on some bandstand one night. Right now I can't imagine that I'll make it to my "golden years" with a bass in my hands. What if I've been delusional? What if I'm aging out of the music business?

Turning Around

2012–2013

"Get a master's in counseling," said Jon, between mouthfuls of eggs Benedict.

"Why counseling and not social work? What about becoming a psychologist?" I asked him.

"If you want to be a therapist, a degree in mental health counseling is the way to go. It's fast, two years, probably. Counseling programs tend to be more clinically oriented than social work schools. And the training to become a psychologist will take you six years, at least."

"OK, I see what you mean. I don't have that kind of time."

Nina and I were having brunch with Jon Lewis, a retired psychiatrist, and his translator wife, Betty DeVise, in late 2012. I'd been itching to ask his advice about this for a while.

"I want to do something purposeful with whatever working life I have left," I said.

"Well," Jon answered. "Counseling would certainly be that. You could make a difference in a lot of people's lives."

"How do I know if I'm cut out for this line of work, though?"

"You won't know until you give it a chance—much like everything else you've ever done."

He had a point there. It was clear to me that, if I sought another means to earn a living, it would have to be something sustainable, a job I could do regardless of physical limitations. I also knew that, after decades of wildly fluctuating income, I longed for a situation with a more reliable paycheck.

The idea of becoming a therapist wasn't completely out of the blue. Way back in high school I'd read books by Erich Fromm, B. F. Skinner, Carl Jung, R. D. Laing, and Fritz Perls. It's possible Korky suggested some of these authors to me. During my aborted final trimester at Northwestern, I'd taken a couple of psychology classes to put some distance between me and the radio/TV/film department. At that age I had no inkling that psychology would ever be more than an academic sideline.

Could I train to work as a therapist at my advanced age and unknown aptitude for anything outside the performing arts? I did some research on master's programs available in Chicago, brainstormed with Nina (who's a clinical social worker), and had that discussion with Jon.

There was a stack of good reasons to transition out of the music biz. More than anything, though, it was doing my own therapeutic work that cracked open the window of curiosity about working in the field. I'd been in and out of therapy since the mid-1980s. Beginning with those relentless, exhausting days at the Hilton, I'd come a long way in understanding how my own psyche ticked. The road had been a bumpy one.

The word "depression" was never spoken during my formative years, though I'm sure everyone in my nuclear family had bouts of it. Without having language for it, when whatever-it-was dragged me into the depths of despair, the only conclusion I could draw was that I was doing life wrong and that I needed to find someone who would tell me how to fix it.

In the mid-1980s, trusted friends recommended a woman who practiced therapy without a license and, I now understand, had terrible interpersonal boundaries. In Illinois, anyone can claim to be a psychotherapist, but only people who've been properly trained and have passed state-sanctioned exams can be granted a license to practice as a clinical social worker, a mental health counselor, a psychologist, or, after going to medical school, a psychiatrist. I knew nothing about any of this then.

"It seems to me your problem is that you're not living enough in the mainstream of things," said this "therapist," who I'll refer to as Deborah. "That's why you're feeling so out of it sometimes."

My bullshit alarm started clanging, but then I did a quick mental about-face.

Well, maybe she's right. It probably is my fault that I feel so crappy so much of the time.

"If that's true, then what do I do about it," I asked Deborah, not particularly wanting to hear her answer.

"Well, maybe you should watch more TV."

I hadn't owned a television for several years by then, which was a point of pride for me. This suggestion made me want to bolt out of her office immediately. But, well-behaved young man that I was, I stayed.

The final straw for me was the session when Deborah told me she listened to Rush Limbaugh every day.

"You ought to give it a try. You might relate to some of the things he says."

Yeah. No. No fucking way was I going to tune in to that asshole.

I left this "treatment" feeling worse about myself than ever.

A competent social worker accompanied me through the cataclysmic period surrounding my divorce, but I didn't have a transformative therapeutic experience until I met Bob Craft. He was a bear of a man, soft spoken, gentle, insightful, and empathic—a calming presence with whom I was finally able to gain some perspective on my emotional life. After seeing him for a few months, I wanted him to tell me if there was a name for the cluster of symptoms that had been gnawing at me on and off for most of my life: low mood, fatigue, irritability, insomnia, poor self-esteem.

"A couple of friends have taken to calling me Mr. Crabbypants," I told Bob. "Which I don't find funny in the least."

"I do think you're dysthymic, yes," Bob said.

"Dis what?"

"Dysthymic. It's the term for someone who's chronically mild-to-moderately depressed."

"And you think that fits me?"

"Yes, I do."

I broke down and wept for the first time in a therapist's office. With that one word, Bob released me from the dark cloud of self-blame I'd been living under for years. The low energy and grumpiness weren't my fault; I wasn't causing my own misery; there was a diagnosis that explained these symptoms.

"Am I a candidate for some kind of medication?" I asked when I was able to compose myself.

"It's possible. Antidepressants are helpful for many people. I'm not qualified to make that call, though. You could certainly arrange a consultation with your doctor. I could also give you a referral to a psychiatrist for an evaluation if you like."

At a subsequent session I asked Bob if we could talk about my lower back pain. "I can't make sense of the timing. Why did it happen so long after that period of intense musical work?"

"Not all stressors are physical," Bob reminds me. "Or obvious or rational."

"Yeah. Hmm."

"What's going on with your life outside of work—your relationships with Nina and your kids?"

"The kids are struggling somewhat with life after college. Things with Nina are good. But—"

"But?"

"Money, man. Always goddamn money. My house is so underwater, the music business is in a tailspin *again*. I don't know if I can hack it much longer. But I can't quit. What would I do?"

"I'm wondering if there's more to it than doubts about your profession."

"Like?"

"Have you ever heard of Erik Erikson's Stages of Psychosocial Development?"

"That's a mouthful. And, no."

"Well, it's a model that divides our lives into eight distinct periods, which follow a certain predetermined order. Look it up sometime. According to Dr. Erikson, you're in the stage he calls generativity versus stagnation."

"Sounds serious."

"Yeah. You can think of it as a fancy way of saying 'midlife crisis.'"

"Well, I did the divorce part. Do I need to buy a red sports car?"

"If only it were that simple. By generativity, Erikson means that it's normal at this time of your life to want to do work that has a meaningful and beneficial impact on society. If you're able to do this successfully, he says, you're more likely to feel a deep sense of purpose and accomplishment."

"Um-kay. Translate that for me?"

"Maybe it's not money that's the real issue here. Could it be that the work you've been doing for the last three decades or so no longer fulfills you the way it used to? That missing energy or mojo or however you think of it, is what Erikson calls stagnation. Not a good feeling at all."

This information packed a wallop. Perhaps the exhaustion, the decreasing tolerance for jobbing, and the recurring back problems all came down to this: being a musician no longer means as much to me as it once did. Maybe the thrill is gone. For good.

A couple of years after my final appointment with Bob I was contemplating a major life shift.

What if I could do for others the kinds of things he did for me?

I hadn't seen the inside of a college classroom in over three decades. *Was my brain still capable of retaining new information? Could I afford it? Would I be able to attend classes and still play my gigs?*

"I don't know you very well, Bill," said Jon as we left the restaurant. "But Nina tells me you've turned things around for yourself many times in the past."

I smiled at Nina.

"I suppose I have."

"If you think about it, I bet there's plenty of overlap between music and counseling. You'll have to immerse yourself in the training and see what happens."

In September 2013 I entered the master's program in mental health counseling at Northeastern Illinois University. The die was cast. Meanwhile, I still had a music career to maintain.

Dinners with Idiots in Restaurants

2013

A Bohemian, two Italians, and a Jew walk into an Italian restaurant. This is not the setup for a joke. This quartet, accurately dubbed the Idiots by Nick's wife Linda, meets here four times a year to celebrate each of our birthdays. We've been doing it for a decade plus. It's the only time the four of us—Jim, Peter, Nick, and me—get together when we aren't playing a gig with one another. These evenings are a couple of hours when we can relax, drink red wine, eat a gigantic meal, gossip about mutual friends, and repeat moldy jokes for the hundredth time. We cap every repast with four Macallans, neat.

It's a congenial group, to be sure, but not without its layers of complexity. Each of us met the others under disparate circumstances but we've all known one another for at least twenty years. Nick is usually affable and has a sharp wit. He can be condescending sometimes, referring to one or the other of us as "Junior" or "Sparky." I'm a personable guy but I sometimes inject a Captain Bringdown vibe to the gig or table. I've explained to my friends that Eeyore is my role model. Jim, a truly talented musician with great ears, is the gullible one. The rest of us are always looking for ways to yank his chain, like the time one of us swapped out his reading glasses with someone else's right before Jim was about to play a set.

"Hey, you guys remember that time when—" Jim starts to say.

"Oh no, here we go," moans Nick.

"You all were sitting at a table and as soon as I sat down, the three of you picked up the table and moved it across the room."

"Yep, we remember," I say. "That was one great day."

Peter is the Big Cheese. We don't talk about it, but the three of us are well aware that we're all his part-time employees. On occasion, Nick hires us to play a show with Linda, who's a kick-ass singer.

Every once in a great while Jim or I might come up with a little giglet. But, though it's a taboo subject, everyone knows Peter is the boss.

At different times, the Idiots have considered adding more folks to our supper club. One time it was another bass player; the other guy was a drummer, who actually did attend one meal. The idea fizzled when we realized that having other people there might ruin the delicate balance we've achieved.

These bacchanals mostly blend together in my memory, but there's one dinner I remember distinctly. In December 2013, while we were celebrating Jim's birthday at our *ristorante normale*, I told my friends I'd just completed my first semester of graduate school.

"Wow, that's super cool," said Nick.

"I always said you were the smart one," added Jim, who's been calling me "Professor" for years. "I had no idea you were in school."

"What are you studying?" asked Nick.

"I'm hoping to earn a master's degree in mental health counseling," I told them.

"Then you'll be able to psychoanalyze us, is that it?" Jim joked.

"Nah, you guys are too far gone to be helped."

Meanwhile, Peter has said nothing.

It didn't register as more than an anomalous blip to me at the time, as we were well into our second bottle of Chianti by then. His silence would only make sense in hindsight.

In the Pits

It takes a moment for my eyes to adjust from the fluorescent glare of backstage to the intimate gloom of the orchestra pit. It's like entering a fortune teller's parlor—hushed and candlelit. All that's missing is the incense, though the pit has its own distinctive aroma, an enigmatic cocktail infused with old coffee and stale sweat. Our musical world lies here, under the boards. Actors prance and sing on the effulgent stage above. Musicians conjure our magic unseen, dressed in black, our bodies melting into the inky darkness of our surroundings.

I wend my way to my corner of the pit, wary of the tangle of power, lighting, and audio cables crisscrossing the carpeted floor. It's between shows during the six-week run of *The Lion King* at Chicago's Cadillac Playhouse in 2015. I've come down here to inspect my arrangement of basses (upright, five-string, and fretless electrics), volume pedals, instrument stands, and cables in the wake of a near-disaster that occurred during the matinee.

Like *Wicked*, the bass book for *The Lion King* has its share of treacherous spots where there's only a few seconds to switch from one bass to another. One number calls for upright for the first third, then a quick change to electric for the remainder. During this afternoon's performance, my upright's endpin (that slender metal shaft protruding from the bottom of basses and cellos) got caught on something as I tried to ditch it in its stand while switching to bass guitar. There was no time to think; my next entrance was a breath away. I set the bass down gingerly atop the confusion of cables and pedals strewn at my feet and made a wild grab for the electric. I got it strapped on just in time to play the next passage. *Man, that was close.*

This blunder was just an unlucky happenstance. But I've been running on fumes for too many of these performances, due to the double life I'm leading these days. It's not quite Clark Kent and Superman, but that's how it sometimes feels.

During the day I'm working as a therapy intern for a nonprofit agency that places its trainees in Catholic parishes. Imagine the culture shock for this nice Jewish boy when he first set foot in one of them! Now I spend two days a week working with clients at two different suburban parishes. Every Thursday I have a full day of individual and group supervision at the agency's office in Hyde Park, which is enlightening but exhausting. Then there's the couple of classes I'm finishing up in my master's program.

There's not much of an opportunity to relax between these two high-stress, high-stakes occupations. And, as I approach my sixtieth birthday, I might have lost a click or two on the energy spectrum.

Certainly, I could have turned down *The Lion King*. If I had, I'd have missed the chance to play a show I'd been wanting to take on for over a decade. I'd watched the movie with my kids umpteen times and never got sick of it. Not only is it a great show, but it had a mystique about it, perhaps because it ran for so long in Chicago and so many top-notch musicians had played it. A few of those people and some of my other favorite musicians had been hired for this iteration of the show. And I couldn't predict what the future would hold for me as I morphed identities. I hoped to be able to continue working as a musician for some years to come, but given the tough time I was having with this run, I began to doubt whether I'd be up for living this dual existence much longer.

Working in the orchestra pit for a Broadway show is lucrative, but the hefty paycheck comes with strings attached: we're expected to perform flawlessly, show after show. A momentary lapse in attention, an instant's loss of precise control of a finger muscle, a sudden equipment failure—the incentive to avoid these kinds of pitfalls is formidable.

When you play eight shows a week there are ample opportunities to make mistakes. As one keyboard player friend of mine bemoans, "It seems like every show I find new ways to fuck up."

Musicians, as well as members of the cast and crew, depend upon one another to be rock solid every performance. Surprises are anathema in this business, as it's all too easy to upset the finely tuned engine that keeps a Broadway show humming along *legato*.

This pressure to perform perfectly feels like a solid ball of anxiety in my gullet. I imagine there's a queue of bass players waiting in the wings, ready to snap up my gig if I mess things up one too many times. Today's gaffe threatened to shove me over the cliff into the abyss of panic.

One major problem was that, when my bass got stuck, I couldn't see a damn thing down there at floor level to unstick it. Black lamps, covered by dark blue gels and clipped to each player's music stand, are the only sources of illumination in the pit. We have to be able to see the music, yes, but anything beyond that is considered gratuitous.

The areas under and behind my stool are veiled in darkness. If I drop anything into that Bermuda Triangle, it's probably gone forever. I imagine there being a vast unseen repository, perhaps in a different dimension, for all the yellow pencils, pink erasers, cough drops, oboe reeds, pocket change, tissues, Post-it notes, reading glasses, flip phones, quill pens, cracker crumbs, tampons, emery boards, rosary beads, and other miscellany musicians have lost in orchestra pits throughout the millennia.

Not only is it dark in the pit, it's dead quiet as well. The floor is carpeted, the walls and ceiling are made of sound-absorbing materials, and there are plexiglass barriers separating the strings, brass, woodwinds, and percussion sections from one another. Each instrument is individually miked, giving the sound engineer absolute control over what's heard through the theater's PA system. *The Lion King's* many voices (soloists and chorus) and our pit orchestra (plus two percussionists playing African instruments from the rafters) must be artfully balanced.

However, the advantages of managing the audio electronically are offset by the loss of the pure unamplified timbres of our instruments. Theatergoers are denied the pleasure of hearing the subtle acoustic properties of horsehair pulling the steel-wound gut string of a violin or the buzzing of lips transformed into the lush fog of a trombone. Or, in my case, the overtone-rich rumblings of my upright bass.

The acoustically dry environment makes it necessary for us to use headphones and a miniature sound-mixing device called an Aviom.

Each player dials in the blend of instruments they prefer. The sound in the pit is so dead that one person often can't hear another who may be just a few feet away. Sometimes I can't even hear myself, except through my headphones, which seems just plain crazy.

Theater musicians are in show business but we're rarely shown. We're only acknowledged in the final seconds of the curtain call—and then by proxy. The conductor, perched high above the proletarian players, enjoys a brief moment in the spotlight. After taking a curt bow, he (it's usually a man but not always) will gesture vaguely in our direction while the audience cranes its collective neck to see what the commotion is about. This well-paid anonymity suits me just fine.

Why would anyone choose this underworld life? Why spend thousands of hours hacking away in a practice room, honing one's craft as a performer, only to hide the results of those efforts in a sub-terranean orchestra pit? For some musicians it's a dream fulfilled, per-haps the result of a childhood spent reveling in Broadway scores by Lerner and Lowe, Rodgers and Hammerstein, or Stephen Sondheim. For others it's a tacit admission of failure, the plan B for an imag-ined career as a concert artist or a member of a major symphony orchestra that never materialized. For me it was a blend of chance and compromise.

During my time at DePaul from 1979 to 1981, I realized that I possessed neither the desire nor the chops to land an orchestra job. And solo concert careers for double bassists are about as rare as Bigfoot sightings. From the moment jazz bassists like Paul Chambers and Charles Mingus grabbed me by the ears in high school, swing-ing a walking bass line was all I wanted to do. Sure, I'd read about the hardscrabble lives of my jazz heroes—the poverty, the constant travel, the drug addiction, the shady record labels, and the shyster club owners.

But somehow I didn't think any of that would apply to me. To a middle-class white kid, it all seemed so romantic—until I dropped out of Northwestern to don a metaphorical beret and join the sub-versive subculture of jazz *artistes*. At the ends of too many subsequent months, those nickel-and-dime jazz gigs in clubs failed to generate enough scratch to pay the rent, fuel the car, or fill the cupboard.

When I received that call inviting me to play eight weeks of *Bye Bye Birdie* at Candlelight Dinner Playhouse in the fall of 1981, I jumped on the opportunity like a drowning man finding a life raft in the middle of the Atlantic. Those weeks turned into nine months and voilà, my theater career had begun. It wasn't jazz—there'd be opportunities for that later—but it was a doorway into the musical career I so desperately wanted.

Sometimes a pit isn't really a pit. The small orchestra for the shows I played at Candlelight, for instance, accompanied the cast from the mezzanine opposite the stage. Instead of lurking in the darkness below, we were hidden in plain sight, directly above and behind the audience. The folks in the seats had to twist their heads all the way around, *Exorcist*-style, to see us.

Ten years later, I played shows from inside a glass cage. At the Lincolnshire Marriott Theater, the orchestra was cooped up in a soundproof glass booth situated behind the seats on one side of that black box theater. The enclosure was so constricted that players had to enter in a prescribed order. Once people nearest the door were seated there was no room to maneuver around them to get anywhere else inside the box. It wasn't an ideal place to work if, like me, you happen to be claustrophobic.

My least favorite pit was essentially a dungeon, minus the leg irons. The brave and underpaid musicians who played *The Three Musketeers* at Chicago Shakespeare Theatre in 2006–2007 were crammed into the trap room below the stage. That's an area normally used either for storage or for some special effect (like a trap door) if one is needed for a particular production. This musty, dim, low-ceilinged room featured vertical support beams, which hindered our view of the conductor and one another. Between the physical conditions, the *fakakta*[1] conductor, and the overwritten score, this show was the nadir of my musical theater life.

In the pit, your sound is your signature, your calling card, your meal ticket. Down there in the murk it's the only thing that truly matters. Classical artists and pop stars entertain audiences visually as well as musically. People tend to listen more with their eyes than

---

1   *Fakakta*: Yiddish for "shitty."

their ears, which is the reason for the tuxedoes and ball gowns in the concert hall as well as the glitter, ball caps, spiked hair, platform shoes, hoodies, or whatever accoutrements are favored by each pop genre.

Musicians of whatever ilk have to be exceptional performers—that's a given. For some artists, though, stagecraft plays as much of a role as the music. Exotic settings, spectacular light shows, multimedia effects, complex choreography, and frequent costume changes are *de rigueur* at many popular music shows. Can you imagine Michael Jackson without the dancing or Lady Gaga without the outrageous outfits? K-Pop is the current prime example of this "music for the eyes" phenomenon.

In stark contrast, theater musicians are heard but not seen. We can't lean on our looks to impress audiences (a blessing for some of us). We dress democratically in basic black. There's no room for choreography or strobe lights in the pit. The criteria for success are 95 percent musical. Do you play with good intonation, phrasing, dynamics, and rhythm? Can you follow the conductor? Are you able to blend your sound with the ensemble? In the pits, there are no visual distractions; no way to hide from the aural truth.

The smell of fresh coffee snaps me back into the present. A few of my colleagues have trickled back to the pit to warm up. There's Bob at the keyboard; Tom in the drum booth; Darlene with her arsenal of ethnic flutes. I hear them and the other orchestra members tooting and noodling. Soon Rick, my favorite music director, will return to the podium. As tired as I am, it's a pleasure like no other to have the privilege of calling these folks my friends and colleagues. I want to savor these moments, especially now that my nights in the pit may be coming to an end.

I root around my area using the powerful industrial flashlight I borrowed from the sound department. It looks as though my upright bass's endpin must have gotten entangled with one of the nearby cables. A couple of those wily snakes have wriggled loose from their duct-taped moorings on the floor. I should have been paying closer attention to the upkeep of my equipment. I've got to be more vigilant if I want to reduce the chances of future potential catastrophes.

I secure all the cables with a double layer of tape and check to make sure all my other tools—bass stands, volume pedals, music stand, Aviom—are firmly anchored in their proper spots. I replace the batteries in both electric basses (I learned *that* lesson years ago.) and check to see that all the cables are connected to their respective pieces of gear. I step back for a final once-over. Everything looks good to go.

Peeking at my phone, I see that the downbeat for the evening performance is twenty minutes away. Excellent. That's just enough time to grab a coffee from the café next door.

In the *Lion King* pit, 2015

Discord, Disunity, Gratitude, and Mercy

September 10, 2017

> There is no single particular noun
> for the way a friendship,
> stretched over time, grows thin,
> then one day snaps with a popping sound.
>
> —Tony Hoagland
> "Special Problems in Vocabulary" (2015)

It had been a day at Unity Church much like every other Sunday for the previous nine and a half years. Every week I had the pleasure of playing electric bass with two of my closest friends, Peter and Sarah. Like any regular job, it had its ups and downs. Our trio performed with a panoply of guest singers, whose level of talent ranged from outstanding to rather, shall we say, modest.

Our trio had outlasted several ministerial regimes. Rev. Erica, equal parts scholar and goofball, hired Peter, then trusted him to hire us in late 2007. She loved dancing to my "Brick House" bass line. Erica had been an actress before entering the ministry, and it was she who instigated an *Always, Patsy Cline* project at Unity in 2008. Playing Patsy's sidekick Louise had been on her bucket list for a long while. With the aid of the extraordinary singer/actress Megon McDonough (who'd played Patsy at Northlight Theater in the original production of the show I played in '97), we helped Erica cross that off before her tragic death from ovarian cancer in 2011.

Rev. Russ, a bitter, angry man about whom the less said the better, followed Erica for two fingernails-on-chalkboard years. Then Rev.

Heidi, a blonde, big-eyed Texan came to Unity. Her theme song was Pharrell Williams's "Happy," which reflects her upbeat personality.

It meant a lot to me that our little band had coalesced as musicians and as friends through all of those changes in church leadership for nearly a decade.

After the day's second service, Peter nodded in my direction, indicating he wanted to have a word with me. As we picked our way down the concrete steps and into the church garden, I surmised that he wanted to commiserate about the musical guest du jour, a singer/guitarist who'd been his usual insolent, pain-in-the-butt self that day. I wagered that Peter had finally reached the end of his rope with him. I certainly had.

Instead, when we reached the edge of the church garden, Peter abruptly stopped walking, turned to face me, and said "I need to make a change." He mumbled something about how this "wasn't personal," that it was "just about business."

Wait, where have I heard this before? Oh, right. The Chicago Hilton and Towers, circa 1991.

He's firing me?

Peter rambled on. He "hoped we could remain friends" and that I'd "continue to play his outside-of-church gigs." It sounded like a speech he'd written on a legal pad and practiced in front of a mirror.

He's firing me.

"Uh, OK," I may have said. I certainly didn't argue with him. I knew any attempt at discussion would go straight to hell. I shouldered my bass guitar and zombie-trudged to my car.

I stared at the steering wheel, waiting for my prefrontal cortex to come back online. Sarah saw me sitting there motionless as she stashed her cymbal bag in her minivan.

"Hey, what's up?" she called.

"Peter just fired me."

"WHAT? WHY?"

I told her the truth: "I have no idea."

We spoke for a few moments, then I drove numbly home.

Over the next few days, I reread an exchange of emails between Peter, Sarah, and me from the previous week. The messages contained a friendly discussion regarding Sarah's and my pay rate for the newly reinstated two-service Sundays. (The church had cut one service for the summer, citing low attendance.) Which left me with one of many mysteries: Why did Peter pretend to care about my paycheck if he knew my days at Unity were about to end?

Compensation for our work at the church had become a perennial issue, because the board of directors was constantly looking for ways to control expenses. The few times the organization had been flush over the years, Peter had encouraged Sarah and I to ask for raises. I was under the (apparently mistaken) impression that he was speaking to us as friends. He later claimed that I was "always complaining about being underpaid" and that these conversations were vexing responsibilities he had to endure as my boss.

Twice during the two years preceding my unexpected firing, Peter had arranged meetings with me to discuss what he viewed as my musical shortcomings on the Unity gig. Each time we met he expressed dissatisfaction with my performance and what he perceived to be my attitude toward the job.

"I don't know how to say this any other way, but it seems to me that you're not committed enough to the music we play at Unity."

"Man, what are you talking about? You send me charts on Wednesday or Thursday, which I play through with the YouTube recordings. If there's anything tricky I take the time to work it out. I show up on time for rehearsals; I'm friendly with everyone, even that asshole guitarist. What am I not doing?"

"Like I said, it's hard to articulate exactly what I'm talking about, but I need you to put more of yourself into the music."

"Now I'm really confused."

"Look, do you even care about music anymore?"

OK, there it is. The exasperated tone of that comment pierced me. Now I knew there was something deeper going on; something that had little or nothing to do with my performance at Unity. I flashed back to that dinner nearly four years ago when Peter gave me the silent treatment after I told the Idiots about starting graduate school.

For several days, I racked my brain trying to understand what had really caused Peter to make this decision. He was the only one of our group who had remained single minded about playing music. Nick had an unrelated day job; Jim was a recording engineer; I taught bass lessons and ran PlayJazzNow. Playing the piano was all Peter had ever wanted to do and all he'd ever done to earn a living. His half-century career was a testament to his talent, hard work, luck, and sheer stubbornness.

It was also, from where I sit, his weakness. By the time of the aforementioned dinner, my friend's life had narrowed precipitously, both personally and professionally. He had lost his comfortable suburban home in a divorce a few years earlier and had moved into a small apartment. The music business, ever hungry for younger and more diverse talent, was presenting him fewer and fewer opportunities. He didn't teach. Though he was an excellent jazz pianist, Peter's musical skill set precluded him from seeking other kinds of work. He'd never learned to read music well enough to work in the theater or sight-read classical music. The upshot was that his part-time job as Unity Church's music director had become Peter's main focus and primary source of income.

Meanwhile, my life was expanding. I, too, had gone through a divorce. However, after a few years of apartment hopping, I was able to purchase another house. I married Nina in 2013. I stitched together a more or less sustainable living from my various musical endeavors, of which the Unity job was but a small patch. When I decided to pursue a master's degree in mental health counseling, I think it blew out Peter's circuits. Was he envious, resentful, frustrated, all of the above? Did he feel betrayed? There was no way to know. He kept his emotions tightly buttoned up in my presence, much as he had done that night at the restaurant.

"You know, the other bass players who sub for you sometimes stand up when we play a high energy number," Peter continued. "I'm not telling you to stand up just because I'm saying you should. I only want you to do it if you feel it."

Well, that's quite a conundrum. I'd never felt like standing and I doubted I ever would. I play bass, fer crissake. The attention should be on the guest artist, not on me. You and Sarah sit, so why would I stand?

I came away from each of these conversations scratching my head, wondering what the hell had just transpired. After each of them, Peter didn't say a word about what I might be doing right or wrong at church. Was I playing too loud or too soft? Too many notes or not enough notes? Did I have the wrong look on my face? Was I really supposed to stand up even if I didn't feel like it? I had no clue whether or not I was meeting Peter's expectations. And he never hinted that my job was in jeopardy if I failed to make these mysterious adjustments.

Until the day he fired me.

I had been closer to Peter than I'd ever been to any other man in my life. He was a mentor, a father figure, the brother I never had. Without realizing it, I'd put my friend on the loftiest of pedestals. I became dependent on him not only for my livelihood but for my self-worth. I felt respected and valued as long as he kept hiring me and treating me like a welcome partner.

Meanwhile, Peter had been holding me in equally unwarranted esteem, projecting feelings of infallibility on me. I was dumbfounded when he revealed how disappointed he was when I committed some all-too-human mistake, such as coming to work overtired and cranky from a tough day or showing up too close to the start time of a job.

Could this fatal breach in our relationship have been avoided? Perhaps. I could have been more forthcoming about my confusion over Peter's intentions during those awful meetings. He could have been more straightforward with his critiques and expectations. I could have expressed my discomfort with the friend/employer duality that none of the Idiots had ever come clean to him about.

There's a chance I could have worked through my hurt and anger to the point of forgiveness. But after the Hilton debacle I swore I would never again allow myself to become dependent on any one person for approbation or my livelihood. Then I let it happen. Again. With the same person.

After the meetings and the firing without warning I knew I was done.

Two Sundays later, I played my last services at Unity. The theme of Rev Heidi's sermon that day was *gratitude*. I had emailed her early in the week, asking her not to announce my departure to the congregation from the pulpit. Getting fired was bad enough; I didn't want to compound the humiliation with some bullshit send-off, something I'd witnessed too many times at that church. Word got around, of course. After the second service a small swarm of folks embraced me and wished me well. When asked why I was leaving I replied that I'd been fired and I didn't really know why—which was as close to the truth as I could get.

I estimate that I played about 850 services during my near-decade working at Unity. That day I felt like just another transient passing through on my way to who-knows-where.

The final tune we played was "Mercy, Mercy, Mercy," which was unintentionally apt. As soon as the last F7 chord faded I went up to Peter, shook his hand, and, in keeping with the day's sermon, simply said, "Thank you."

The Pillars Crumble

Jobbing. Theater. Jazz. Teaching. All four pillars of my musical life came tumbling down in the last quarter of 2017.

The demise of the Unity gig had an unfortunate coda: since most of the jobbing I'd been doing at that time was with Peter, a clutch of one-nighters disappeared from my calendar along with all those Sunday mornings. It was rather late in the year to start booking jobs with other people, like Christmas parties and New Year's Eve. I would have had to go trolling for gigs by calling bandleaders and bass player colleagues, something I didn't have the emotional wherewithal to do.

Though I didn't realize it at the time, I was grieving. It was all I could do to keep my shit together enough to see my clients.

I reluctantly turned down six lucrative weeks of *Wicked* for December and January. I knew that neither my chops nor my head were in any kind of shape to take on a commitment of that difficulty. It had been six years since my last trial by fire with that show. My chops were in noticeably worse condition now. The arthritis in the joints of my index finger and the chronic lower back pain were worse, my physical stamina was diminished because I'd been playing so few gigs, and my schedule as a psychotherapist was busier than ever.

More importantly, my priorities had shifted. My therapy clients deserved my full attention. Piling eight shows a week on top of my caseload would leave me too exhausted to be an effective clinician or a competent musician. Rather than bull my way through a potentially disastrous situation, I chose self-preservation.

In lieu of playing *Wicked*, I accepted a two-week run of *White Christmas* at the Cadillac Playhouse Theater right around Thanksgiving. I was skeptical about this gig too, but Tim, the con-tractor, was persuasive. I convinced myself that two weeks of a less strenuous show would be possible, maybe even pleasant. Some of my favorite musicians would be in the pit; the book called for upright bass only and looked pretty easy; and putting five grand in my pocket wouldn't be bad either.

Man, was I wrong. I'd forgotten how much energy-zapping concentration is required to play a show at a high level of professionalism. I severely underestimated the physical stress even doing an "easy" show would inflict on my body. Fun was out of the question. Those two weeks were a survival test.

Despite the heartbreaking loss of my relationship with Peter, the worsening physical ailments, and my increasing responsibilities as a therapist, I fantasized that I'd continue to play gigs of my choosing for some time to come. I imagined a grand, well-orchestrated crossfade between my two professions where, over the course of several years, I'd establish a thriving private psychotherapy practice and gradually accept fewer and fewer music jobs.

Like I said, it was a fantasy.

At the end of 2017, I informed my remaining handful of students that I was retiring from teaching. Then, as 2018 unfurled, I found I was only getting intermittent calls for gigs I either couldn't or didn't want to do. January and February of that year were colder and snowier than normal, which made me disinclined to leave the house for anything other than going to the office.

Weeks went by, then months. My practice was growing steadily. I was no longer at the mercy of the almighty phone or email inbox. Counseling is a freelance business, much as music is, but the former isn't subject to the whims of fate and the health of the economy nearly as much as the latter.

Mental health counseling was feeling more and more like home, where I was supposed to be. The work was by no means easy. I knew I still had a lot to learn but, as one of my grad school profs told my cohort, "Your clients will be your best teachers"—like my musical mentors Korky, Wayne, Ed, Joe Daley, Peter, Dave Holland, et al.—had been. Practicing psychotherapy connected me deeply with each of my clients, much as playing music had connected me with my fellow musicians.

"So, Saturday night and no gig. What do you think about that?" I asked Nina in the spring.

"Hah, well, what do *you* think of it?"

"It's taken some getting used to, but I think I'm managing the reflexive guilt pretty well. I never got why people liked having their nights and weekends free so much."

"Yeah, it's pretty cool."

"I always thought the subversive lifestyle of musicians was the only way to live. Guess I was wrong. It only took me forty years to figure that out."

In November 2018, Tim offered me the chance to play two weeks of the musical version of *How the Grinch Stole Christmas*. It was tempting to go for a last hurrah and a wad of cash. I accepted the gig and picked up the music from Tim.

I set up my practice room to feel much like my space in the pit would probably feel. Upright and electric bass at the ready, music stand with my iPad mounted on top (so I could watch a video of the music director conducting the show), headphones, a little practice amp. Halfway through the first act my body began to complain. I dragged myself through the rest of the show, by the end of which I'd made a decision and left a message for Tim:

"Hey, Tim, Bill Harrison calling. Listen man, I don't think I can make the *Grinch* gig. I remember you telling me that the producers wanted to squeeze twenty shows out of us in fourteen days, and I'm pretty sure I can't handle that, physically or mentally. I hate to pass up the dough, of course, but I don't want to crash and burn and create a bad situation for all concerned. So sorry, man. I hope you can find someone else to play the book. OK, later. Thanks."

Tim graciously found another bassist to play the show. A few months later, when I knew in my bones I was no longer capable of working in the theater, he and I exchanged emails:

February 7, 2019, 11:27 a.m.

Hi, Tim,

It looks as if for all intents and purposes I'm retiring from the music business. Between my new career and the physical problems I've been experiencing for the last couple of years it seems like the best course of action to follow.

So, I'm writing to say thank you for inviting me to perform so many times for so many shows, both traveling and local. I appreciate the faith you've shown in my abilities and wanted to let you know how grateful I am for all of those opportunities.

Best wishes to you and your family. I hope to see you around the theater 'hood as a civilian. I do go to see a show once in a while :-)

Bill

February 7, 2019, 11:47 a.m.

Hey, Bill.

Thanks for your note. It's been a pleasure to have you on those shows. You always sounded terrific, and I've always loved your feel. Best wishes for continued success in the new career, and great health.

Cheers,
Tim

WWKD

December 14, 2017

"Park your car, sir?" the valet at the Hotel Palomar asks as I emerge from my vehicle.

"Sure," I tell him. "I just need a minute to unload my music gear. I've got an engagement here tonight."

"Take your time, sir."

Wow, someone treating me, a musician, like an actual human being. Will wonders never cease.

I'm about to play what looks to be a low-key cocktail party with Fred and Sarah, two of my oldest friends and colleagues. I don't know this for certain, but I suspect this may be my final gig of the year. My book is completely white, gig-wise, from here on out.

Korky has been on my mind lately. One of my high school buddies must have mentioned his name recently. Images of him return as I set up my bass guitar and amp, then find a cushy armchair to relax in before the gig. My old friend and mentor dropped out of mainstream life decades ago, having suffered a debilitating mental disorder. No one seems to know the diagnosis; I imagine there's an element of psychosis in the picture but have little basis for that assumption, other than bits and pieces of info I've picked up over the years.

A half century has passed since those afternoons digging Albert Ayler and Cecil Taylor sides in Korky's bedroom. Had it not been for his willingness to share his enthusiastic embrace of jazz with me, I don't believe I would have chosen music as my life's work. I wouldn't be here right now, about to play this gig with my friends.

When faced with confusion and indecision in my earliest years as a musician, I'd often wonder: *What would Korky do in this situation?* I've grown less dependent on that internal question, but it has popped up on occasion throughout my career.

I wish you were here, my friend. I wish we could talk music once again.

Fred and Sarah arrive. I *kibbitz* with them as they set up keys and drums. Once they're ready, our trio plays Vince Guaraldi's version of "O Christmas Tree" to begin the evening. My attention is split between the gig and musings about Korky. This situation evokes echoes of that first bowling alley job I played with him and Ted. The gigs aren't similar in any way except the warm feelings I had then and have now when I'm playing music with good friends.

I wish to hell Korky and I could spirit ourselves back to 1974 for one last jam session. We'd do what we did then: play the craziest, go-for-broke shit for an hour then collapse from emotional and physical exhaustion. I would love to reexperience the exhilaration of making music with one of the most remarkable and creative people I've ever known.

I draw my mind back to the here and now, to this gig, to these friends. We're playing for a congenial group of people, many of whom know Sarah. So we get an unusual amount of attention and a smattering of applause now and then. At the end of our last set we finish with a chorus of "The Christmas Song" as a gentle ballad. The three of us are certain we won't see one another until next year, so there are hugs and fond "see ya laters" as we pack up our equipment and head home.

Back in the solitude of my car, I can't help thinking of Korky again. He has been gone from my life for four decades. I just lost another hugely influential friend and mentor in Peter. There's the whiff of finality in the cold air.

As it happens, not only was this gig with Fred and Sarah my last of 2017, it was also the last performance of my career.

Leading from Behind

> Artists are people driven by the tension between the desire to communicate and the desire to hide.
>
> —D. W. Winnicott
> *Playing and Reality*, 1971

Sometimes, in the middle of a Zoom session with a counseling client, I sense the presence of my Amelot bass nestled behind me in a corner of my office. On occasion, I will coax a few notes from it. Nowadays, this magnificent old soul of an instrument serves both as a witness to my past self and as a touchstone for my present self.

For the first half century of my life, I was convinced that all my doubts, fears, anxieties, and shame would disappear if only I could devise a cohesive, all-encompassing, logical autobiographical narrative. Lord knows I tried, on my own and with several unsuspecting therapists. I longed to uncover incontrovertible evidence—a video my guardian angel had been shooting since my birth, say, like a benign version of *The Truman Show*—that would make sense of everything and give me peace of mind once and for all.

In my mid-fifties, I began to suspect this quest was a fool's errand. It wasn't until I became a psychotherapist in 2015 that I realized how impossible and undesirable this goal was. *Homo sapiens sapiens* is a meaning-making species. Our memories are unreliable, capricious, subjective. But we need those mutable interpretations of past events to form our personalities, to grow, to become who we are now and who we will be in the future. The ways our minds encode memories allow us to reimagine and reconstruct them. This is a feature, not a bug. It's the basis for emotional healing which, in turn, is the endgame of therapy.

I no longer have callouses on my fingers; the strength and dexterity it took me years to develop are gone. Arthritic pain in the knuckles of my left index finger and a misshapen pinkie are the only physical vestiges of my former life. But the psychological remains are powerful: forty years of mental and emotional development that has somehow, through no conscious intention of my own, made it possible to put my core inner conflict—a fear of being seen and a simultaneous yearning to be seen—to generative use in my work as a mental health counselor.

As Jon the psychiatrist had suggested, the practices of psychotherapy and music have much in common. Both blend theory with artistry, require vigilant attention to detail, and depend on collaboration and mutual trust. No trait is more crucial in both disciplines than empathy, the ability to attune to the present-moment emotional experience of another person.

Bass players are particularly well suited to connect with others in this intimate way. Bassists "lead from behind" by generating the harmonic and rhythmic context for our ensemble-mates. We build the foundation upon which our more extroverted peers can stand and strut their stuff. The bass is the most self-effacing of instruments; it's the gentle giant behind the guitars, fiddles, singers, horn players, and anyone else who makes a joyful noise. All the while, bassists are tuned in to the details of the music and the people making it. We're poised to adjust and accommodate at a moment's notice. Our contributions, however subtle, can make or break a performance.

Empathic connection is also one of the fundamental tools therapists use to create and strengthen the therapeutic relationship we have with each of our clients. We listen carefully and respond thoughtfully. Counselors walk with their clients like good sidemen, hold up a mirror to them, and observe their patterns of thoughts, feelings, and behaviors—all in the service of encouraging positive change. We don't tell people how to resolve their issues or offer advice. We provide the environment in which self-awareness can increase and potential resolutions to long-term problems can arise.

The model of counseling I use (psychodynamic psychotherapy, if you want the "teshnical" term) acknowledges that my role is to be fully engaged with the other person without being the center of attention.

Much like playing the bass, it's an ideal level of involvement for me. I work to foster the process, present but out of the spotlight. Leading from behind.

The bass in the corner of my office is my anchor. It tethers me to my roots, reminds me to listen beyond the words and to respond with compassion and humility. It encourages me to be my spontaneous self, to know that what I brought to music and what I bring to counseling is enough.

Acknowledgments

The following chapters were previously published in slightly different forms in these journals: "A Duck Among Penguins" in *Under the Gum Tree*; "In the Pits" in *The Sandpiper*; "La Contrebasse Francais" in *After Hours*.

Way back in 2006, a good friend by the name of Helena Bouchez encouraged me to start sharing my writing on an ancient electronic papyrus called Blogspot. She has been an inspiration in so many ways ever since. Thank you, HB.

My sincere thanks to the group of friends who encouraged my daily writing practice by agreeing to receive an email every day for ten months with each day's scribblings. The raw material I generated during that period became the basis for this book.

Special thanks to the friends who offered valuable feedback on the manuscript at various stages: David Van Biema, Kevin McMullin, Lloyd King, and Jack Kassel.

Extraordinary thanks to my writing partner, the uber-talented Jaymee Martin.

I'm grateful to the wise and patient creative writing teachers I was lucky to study with as this project took shape: Dina Elenbogen, Joelle Fraser, Meghan O'Gieblyn, and Kase Johnstun.

Voluminous gratitude to the editors who helped me whip this thing into shape: Sarah Valentine, Debbie Burke, and the estimable Shelley Sperry, without whom this book probably wouldn't exist.

Super-duper gratitude to Jennifer Geist, publisher of Open Books Press, who was willing to take a chance with a first-time author.

Finally, extra special thanks with a cherry on top to my wife and first reader, poet and master psychotherapist Nina Corwin.

About the Author

Bill Harrison worked as a professional bassist in Chicago for four decades. He performed with jazz luminaries Clark Terry, James Moody, Bunky Green, Max Roach, Woody Herman's Thundering Herd, Dizzy Gillespie, and many others. His theatrical credits include *Wicked*, *The Lion King*, *Always Patsy Cline*, *The Visit*, *Bounce*, *Turn of the Century*, and *Billy Elliot*. Bill's writing has been published in *After Hours*, *Allium*, *Counseling Today*, *The Intermezzo*, *Performink*, *The Sandpiper*, *Sledgehammer*, *Under the Gum Tree*, and elsewhere. He has a private psychotherapy practice in Chicago, where he lives with his poet/therapist wife and a naughty Bengal named Jazzy.

CPSIA information can be obtained
at www.ICGtesting.com
Printed in the USA
JSHW061205081222
34471JS00003B/171